Investment Climate
Around the World

Voices of the Firms from the
World Business Environment Survey

DIRECTIONS IN DEVELOPMENT

Investment Climate Around the World

*Voices of the Firms from the
World Business Environment Survey*

Geeta Batra, Daniel Kaufmann, and Andrew H.W. Stone

THE WORLD BANK
Washington, D.C.

© 2003 The International Bank for Reconstruction and Development / The World Bank
1818 H Street, NW
Washington, DC 20433
Telephone 202-473-1000
Internet www.worldbank.org
E-mail feedback@worldbank.org

ISBN 0-8213-5390-X

Library of Congress Cataloging-in-Publication Data has been applied for.

Contents

Tables

Foreword

Successful development depends largely on private initiative, including that of entrepreneurs and firms, to invest and produce in urban and rural areas. The extent to which these investments are made depends principally on their expected returns and associated risks. Entrepreneurship is everywhere, particularly among poor people. It is the climate in which they have to operate that can frustrate their efforts.

There is an unfortunate perception that work to improve conditions for private sector development does not relate to poverty alleviation and social development. We know at the end of the day that growth is the key driver for poverty reduction. Growth is not the whole story; there is also the key challenge of empowering people to participate in that growth and investing in them. But growth is central, and we know that in a broad sense the investment climate and business environment are central to growth.

The investment climate depends on a large number of factors, including three main blocks—the macroeconomy, institutions, and infrastructure—and covers much of the structural agenda of the World Bank. When designing a country program we should always ask ourselves whether we are doing enough to help our clients build the appropriate investment climate. That question is a lens through which to evaluate our programs—a way to organize and prioritize our country programs.

Given the comprehensive and cross-cutting nature of the investment climate, better coordination within the development community is key. Good analysis at the country level is needed to establish priorities for improving conditions for efficient investment and improved market competition. A standard diagnostic instrument applied uniformly across countries would provide powerful support to planners and policymakers drafting reform strategy.

In this context, the World Business Environment Survey (WBES) and this global report on its findings provide an ideal starting point. Before the WBES was launched through the World Bank Group's Innovation Marketplace in 1998, approaches to evaluating investment climate conditions were uneven and rarely generated comparable cross-country indicators. The great contribution of this initiative, then, was to prove the value of a coordinated and consistent approach to measuring the investment climate, and to provide practical policy implications for the 80 countries studied. The empirical work in this volume confirms the value of this approach through the insights it provides on policy priorities of the private sector and the contributing conditions to firm-level growth and formal participation in the economy. This, in turn, has laid the groundwork for deepening and expanding survey-based approaches to comparative evaluation as the Bank's focus on the investment climate has intensified.

The value of investment climate assessment lies not merely in a one-time cross-country look at relative conditions, but also in repeating such assessments over time. Consistent measurement of conditions over time should provide an invaluable guidepost to the ongoing efforts of developing countries to strengthen their policy and institutional conditions for private-led growth.

Nicholas Stern
Chief Economist
The World Bank Group

Acknowledgments

Andrew Stone and Geeta Batra served as task managers and Daniel Kaufmann was a core member of the steering committee of the World Business Environment Survey (WBES), which was made possible by a grant from the 1998 Innovation Marketplace. WBES reflects a collaboration across units of the World Bank Group—in particular, Development Economics (DEC), the Foreign Investment Advisory Service (FIAS), the International Finance Corporation, Poverty Reduction and Economic Management (PREM), Private Sector and Infrastructure (PSI), and the World Bank Institute (WBI)—and a collaboration among organizations—in particular, the European Bank for Reconstruction and Development (EBRD), the International Development Bank, and Harvard University. WBES was overseen by a steering committee that included this book's authors as well as Guy Pfeffermann, Homi Kharas, Shyam Khemani, and Luke Haggarty. The survey would not have been possible without the support of the Bank's president, James. D. Wolfensohn; members of the World Bank board of directors; sponsors Nemat Shafik, Alan Gelb, Luis Guasch, Richard Newfarmer, Paul Collier, Mark Baird, and Magdi R. Iskander; and the special contributions of Shyam Khemani, Guy Pfeffermann, and, more recently, Joseph Battat, Michael Klein, and Axel Peuker. Collaborators on regional, country, analytical, or resource efforts included Brian Levy, Hamid Alavi, Ronnie Das Gupta, Su Yong Song, Djordjija Petkoski, Karin Millett, David Sewell, Dale Weigel, Roumeen Islam, Aart Kraay, Bernard Drum, Massimo Mastruzzi, William Rex, and Jacques Morisset. Our external partners included Joel Hellman, Steven Fries, and Mark Shankerman of EBRD; Eduardo Lora of the Inter-American Development Bank (IADB); Sara Sievers of the Harvard Center for International Development; and Samiha Fawzy of the Egyptian Center for Economic Studies. The authors also thank Misha Belkindas for comments on an earlier draft. This book was supported by a grant from the Swiss government and by joint funding from the FIAS, the Private Sector Advisory Services Department (Investment Climate Unit), the WBI, and the Innovation Marketplace. The authors thank Massimo Mastruzzi, Nithya Nagarajan, and Jean Pascal Nganou for their contribution to data analysis and presentation.

About the Authors

Daniel Kaufmann is the director for global governance and for capacity enhancement at the World Bank Institute (WBI). Regarded as a leading expert and adviser in the field of governance, he has published widely on academic and policy issues, pioneering new empirical and survey methodologies with colleagues at the World Bank and in academic settings. He and his team support countries that request governance and anti-corruption assistance in their efforts to improve governance through a rigorous empirical, systemic, and strategy-driven approach.

Kaufmann frequently advises state leaders, senior officials, and civil society on strategies to improve governance and address corruption. Previously he held positions as senior manager for governance, regulation, and finance, WBI; lead economist in the development economics group; and chief of mission of the Bank in Ukraine in the early to mid-1990s. He was a core team member in producing the *World Development Report 1991*, which distilled the key lessons from development experience.

As a visiting scholar at Harvard University in the mid-1990s, Kaufmann provided policy advice on a range of economic and institutional issues to governments in emerging economies. He has published extensively in the leading economic and public policy journals on issues of economic development, privatization, governance, the unofficial economy, industrial and trade restructuring, corruption, transparency, and urban and labor economics.

A Chilean national, Kaufmann received his Ph.D. and master's degrees in economics at Harvard University, and a bachelor of science degree in economics and statistics from the Hebrew University of Jerusalem.

Geeta Batra is senior private sector development specialist in the Foreign Investment Advisory Service (FIAS) of the Private Sector Advisory Services Group. Her main areas of work include research, technical assistance, and policy analysis on projects related to productivity, private sector skills upgrading, competitiveness, FDI flows, and assessments of the business environment and investment climate, with experience in many developing countries. Batra has published articles in the *Journal of International Economics, International Journal of Industrial Organization, World Bank Economic Review,* and the *Journal of Development Economics.* She has a Ph.D. in economics from Pennsylvania State University, where her research focused on international trade, development, and econometrics.

Andrew H. W. Stone is a senior private sector development specialist in the Investment Climate Unit of the Private Sector Advisory Services Department of the World Bank. He is currently program manager for Investment Climate Assessments, a new instrument designed to provide a standard and comparable basis for assessing private enterprise operation and growth. At the Bank he has worked on both the methods for assessing the investment climate through enterprise surveys and policy analysis and the application of those methods in a variety of countries. His survey work has pioneered the assessment of costs to private enterprises of regulatory and administrative compliance. In addition, his work concerns redressing constraints to private sector development, including the identification and application of appropriate institutional approaches to regulatory reform. As part of the Investment Climate Unit, Stone works to promote standard approaches to assessing the investment climate in World Bank member countries through uniform survey instruments, sampling methodology, and indicators, and through adaptations required to capture the experience of small enterprises and those in rural areas. He has managed a research project on business–government consultative mechanisms and their impact on economic governance, and he managed the World Business Environment Survey, which was carried out in 80 countries and one territory. Stone is author or coauthor of several articles, Bank discussion papers, and Web-based resources on private sector development, business transactions costs, and empirical evaluation of business constraints.

Introduction and Summary

Background: Listening to Firms Is Important

How can one assess and compare the environments for doing business and investing in countries around the world? If private enterprises are a critical path out of poverty[1] through employment or ownership, then establishing business environment conditions associated with their growth (within the official economy) must be a key component of a poverty-reduction strategy. The World Business Environment Survey (WBES), using a uniform core questionnaire administered in roughly parallel fashion to enterprises in 80 countries and one territory, provides a basis for regional comparisons of investment climate and business environment conditions, and comparisons of the severity of constraints that affect enterprises according to characteristics, such as size or ownership. It also permits some evaluation of conditions in specific countries.[2] It captures companies' perceptions of key constraints in the business environment—perceptions that shape operational and investment decisions—as well as several quantitative indices of companies' experiences.

The survey results are particularly important in the context of economic globalization. Against a backdrop of growing competition and globalization, member countries increasingly are concerned about how conducive the business environment is to private investment and business development, and they want to know their relative standing regionally or globally. It is unfortunate that very few indicators support objective measurement and comparison of the business environment, its binding constraints, and the quality and integrity of supportive and regulatory public services. There are no adequate benchmarks to establish a basis for understanding the change in the severity of constraints and the quality of business services over time. The WBES was created to fill that gap.

This book presents and analyzes the WBES responses of more than 10,000 firms. The analysis confirms the clear importance of a few key country conditions for company growth and investment: financing problems, high taxes, corruption, policy uncertainty, and insufficient business

1

consultation. Taken together, those conditions can make a difference in firm-level sales and investment growth of almost 11 percentage points. Results also show that informality (hiding revenue) is positively associated with macroeconomic constraints (such as inflation and exchange rate uncertainty), regulatory and tax constraints, corruption, and weak protection of intellectual property rights.

Chapters two and three provide the first comprehensive summary of the major patterns and findings of the global WBES results. Most constraints are presented by region and many by firm size, focusing in particular on the findings regarding reported constraints imposed by policy instability and uncertainty; taxes and regulations; inflation/price instability and the exchange rate; finance; governance, the legal system and corruption; and the quality of public services, including infrastructure. The analysis in this report is based on a sample of 10,032 enterprises that responded to the core questionnaire.

With empirical analysis of that rich enterprise dataset, in chapter four we provide a selective analysis of key determinants of firm performance and their behavior. We suggest which constraints most profoundly affect firm-level outcomes. Also, we explore what types of firms are affected by what business constraints. The close nexus of the investment climate for business development and governance is a significant theme throughout this work.

Considerable effort has gone into analysis of the survey data, both by the book's authors and by others.[3] We present some key findings and provide for further reference a bibliography of publications that have used this dataset. Arguably, however, the more valuable contribution of this work may reside simply in presenting, explaining, and making accessible to analysts, academics, and students this worldwide enterprise dataset.

The main text of the report includes detailed explanations of the data, many of them summarized graphically. Detailed tables in the book's two extensive annexes feature the survey instrument and data for each country and region for most key variables.[4] And the CD-ROM enclosed with this volume provides the core WBES dataset, an interactive tool for analyzing results, and a link to other Web-based resources. The dataset reflects the ambitious, multipartner effort that has gone into conducting this survey of firms on all continents, as well as into processing the data and integrating results into a unified dataset.

Main Findings on Overall Constraints to Enterprise

When we focus on a simple average for the overall world sample, the following constraints to enterprise stand out: taxes and regulations, financing, policy instability and uncertainty, and inflation. Such worldwide average results, however, mask crucial differences across regions, and particularly between industrial and developing countries. In countries in the Organisation for Economic Co-operation and Development (OECD), newly industrialized East Asian countries, and transition economies, firms identified those constraints as the leading obstacles. In developing regions (that is, countries in Africa, Latin America and the Caribbean [LAC]; the Middle East and North Africa [MENA]; South Asia; and East Asia), however, the leading constraint is corruption, followed by inflation, financing, policy instability, and infrastructure. In four developing regions—South Asia, Africa, developing East Asia, and MENA—corruption figures as one of the three leading constraints. Salient regional differences emerge. For example, in South Asia street crime imposes the leading constraint, but in Africa infrastructure is identified as the second-leading problem after financing. In Central and Eastern Europe (CEE), inflation ties with taxes and regulations as the leading constraints. The large regional (and country-centered) variance in severity assigned by responding firms to the constraints points to the importance of assessing the results by region and country, rather than relying on worldwide averages.

Size Matters in Complex Ways

A detailed reading of the data suggests the complex interaction of firm characteristics with business environment conditions. For example, corruption is seen as more constraining by smaller and younger firms, by those with government or public ownership, and by those that export. An inadequate exchange rate regime appears to be felt more by medium-size firms, younger firms, and those with some state ownership.

The data also indicate that for most categories of obstacles, small and medium enterprises (SMEs) identify themselves as more constrained than larger firms.[5] Indeed, in reviewing the many key potential obstacles to business development, the econometric evidence suggests that firms that are private, smaller, newer, devoid of foreign direct investment (FDI), and that cater to the domestic market generally tend to report more acute business constraints than do firms that are older, larger, that export, that have FDI, or that are state-owned. There are notable exceptions regarding some business constraints, however. For instance, older firms report being more constrained by political instability than do younger firms, and exporters are more likely to be constrained by inflation than are nonexporters. For obvious reasons exporters are hit harder by an inadequate exchange rate regime than are nonexporters. SMEs report being more constrained than large firms along most dimensions.

Among SMEs, small firms generally are more constrained than are medium-size firms, perhaps because the objective conditions of relatively larger firms are better or because they can better cope with constraints. But an exploration of the full results also gives rise to the notion of the *for-*

gotten middle. This finding challenges the orthodoxy that claims invariably the smaller the firm, the more severe the constraint. In facing some obstacles to doing business, medium-size firms identify themselves as equally or even more constrained than do small firms.[6] In particular, medium-size firms show no statistical difference from small firms in their rating of several general constraints and are significantly more likely to be seriously constrained by tax administration and infrastructure. With regard to infrastructure, large firms show a statistically significantly higher degree of constraint than do SMEs. These results suggest that policy interventions unduly focused on microenterprises, on small enterprises, or on both may overlook important constraints to medium-size enterprises or all private enterprises. The complexity characterizing the way in which different obstacles appear to affect different types of enterprises reinforces the rationale for focusing on across-the-board reduction of obstacles to businesses, rather than for (the often unproductive) targeting of policies according to firms' characteristics, such as size.[7]

Specific Business and Investment Climate Constraints

Taxes and Regulations

Taxes and regulations impose a severe constraint. They top the constraint list in countries of the OECD, in Latin America, and in transition economies (CEE and members of the Commonwealth of Independent States [CIS]). By contrast, taxes and regulations were rated as a much less significant constraint in Africa, in East Asian developing and newly industrialized countries, and in MENA countries. The survey asked firms to evaluate the severity of a list of potential regulatory constraints. In every region, high taxes topped this regulatory list. Independent of the direct cost of tax payments, tax administration imposes a major or moderate constraint for more than 70 percent of firms in Central and Eastern Europe, 65 percent of firms in CIS countries, and 63 percent of firms in LAC. Customs procedures and trade regulations impose serious constraints for more than half of all firms in LAC and South Asia, but are less severe in other regions. The degree of constraint imposed by labor regulations varies sharply by region, with about 60 percent of South Asian firms and more than 50 percent of Latin American firms finding labor regulations to be a major or moderate constraint. The impact is lower in other regions.

Finance

The second-leading general constraint for the global sample was financing. Firms in Central and Eastern Europe were most likely to identify it as seriously constraining, followed by those in CIS countries, and then those in Africa, South Asia, and LAC. Globally, although financing is identified as the second-leading constraint by SMEs, it ranked fourth for large enterprises. Consistent with findings from surveys of this nature, high interest rates were reported to be a leading financial constraint across all regions, followed by access to long-term credit. Sources of finance vary markedly by region and firm size. Internal funds and retained earnings provide the leading source of financing across regions, but in South Asia and LAC domestic commercial banks provide 20 percent of investment finance, and in developing East Asia and OECD nations, banks provide about 15 percent. In Africa, where financing sources were measured differently, self-financing and internal funds were cited most commonly, followed by the firm's own capital or equity. By size, SMEs in the sample relied less on commercial and foreign banks for investment finance than did large firms, and they depended more on internal funds and retained earnings.

Policy Uncertainty and Instability

At one extreme, more than 70 percent of firms in South Asia, Central and Eastern Europe, and the developing countries of East Asia reported policy instability as seriously constraining, with firms in Latin America, MENA, and CIS close behind. By contrast, only 26 percent of firms in newly industrial countries of East Asia (East Asia NIC/China) identified this constraint as major or moderate, and only 37 percent of firms in OECD countries did so. Firms differed by region in the particular dimension of policy instability that troubled them. More than 70 percent of firms in CEE, more than 60 percent of firms in CIS countries and developing countries in East Asia, and about half the firms in LAC considered economic and financial policies to be unpredictable. In CEE and Africa, nearly three-quarters of firms rated changes in rules, laws, and regulations affecting them as unpredictable; two-thirds of firms in CIS countries shared that assessment. Sixty-eight percent of firms in CEE, 60 percent of CIS firms, and 57 percent of Latin American firms responding reported that they were seldom or never notified in advance of changes affecting them. Finally, in the transition economies of CIS and CEE countries, MENA, and LAC, the majority of firms reported that government rarely considered businesses' views when formulating legal and policy changes.

Corruption and Governance

Corruption was identified as a serious constraint by more than 70 percent of firms in South Asia and by nearly as many in developing countries of East Asia and MENA. Sixty-four percent of firms in Africa, almost 60 percent of those in LAC, and about half in CIS countries and in CEE reported it as a serious impediment. That result contrasts with the much lower share (about 20 percent) of firms in East Asia NIC/China,[8] and in OECD countries that rate corruption as a major or moderate obstacle. Furthermore, in many of the developing countries the majority of firms reported that it was common "in their line of business to have to pay some irregular 'additional payments' to get things done." The data on the reported percentage of total revenue that firms pay every year in bribes clearly and positively correlates with the data on the degree to which firms find corruption constraining. Capture is another important form of corruption, and is negatively associated with firm growth (see box I.1).

An important sign of weak governance is the extent to which registered firms operate unofficially, and related, the degree to which firms comply with tax laws. While there are variations from region to region, about one-half of the firms indicated reporting no more than 80 percent of their revenues.

Quality of Public Services

About two-thirds of firms in Central Europe, Latin America and the Caribbean, and CIS countries, and nearly 60 percent of firms in South Asia reported that the government is inefficient in delivering services. The rate of dissatisfaction is particularly marked among smaller firms. There is variation in the evaluation of different types of public services and institutions: on average, the majority of firms gave a negative rating to public health, parliament, and public works/roads, and more than 40 percent negatively rated the courts, police, education services, and central government leadership. By contrast, the postal, telephone, and electric power services were the most positively rated services.

Business Environment, Investment Climate, Governance, and Enterprise Performance

Direct reporting on the main constraints to enterprise development perceived by firms is now recognized as an increasingly valuable tool for assessing a country's business climate. The information given directly by firms, notwithstanding the element of subjectivity and margin of error, generally is found to be highly correlated with other measures and provides a sound basis for assessing the business and governance climate.[9] At the same time, additional insights emerge when such direct reporting of constraints is complemented by econometric analysis that evaluates whether and how business environment variables affect a firm's performance. An econometric analysis suggests that, controlling for other factors, firms in countries with poor conditions in the areas of finance, high taxes, corruption, and policy predictability, as measured by survey indi-

---

Box I.1 State Capture in Transition Economies: A Major Manifestation of Misgovernance

Traditional measures of corruption derived from enterprise survey questions are useful to assess the extent to which administrative bribery is present in a particular country, and thereby the extent of bribery provides an indicator of the extent to which corruption exists in the *implementation* of laws and regulations. The transition economy version of the WBES (the "BEEPS" survey) went further and assessed the extent to which countries may have experienced good or poor governance in shaping policies, laws, and regulations. Such research revealed that in about half of the countries in transition (particularly those in the CIS, but also some in CEE), there had been a great degree of state capture by the corrupt interests of the enterprise elite. In those countries, the policies, laws, and regulations of the state are reported to have been shaped significantly by some firms' corrupt payments. The empirical work further indicates that the effect of misgovernance characterized as state capture on the business and investment climate is very large: firms in countries that avoided state capture grew much faster and invested significantly more than did those subject to state capture. The implications of this work go beyond the need to monitor and measure this important manifestation of "grand corruption" (typically not measured). The policy implication is if indeed some firms are not merely investment climate "takers," but also investment climate "makers," conventional advice to government officials about what rules and regulations should be reformed will have limited impact in those settings subject to state capture by the vested interests of the elite. For background research and interactive access to the data: http://info.worldbank.org/governance/beeps/.

---

cators, experienced an average sales growth rate of 10.5 percentage points less than did those with positive ratings in all of these categories over a three-year period. A second test explores the factors associated with firm-level investment growth reported over a three-year period (generally 1996–98 or 1997–99). Among business environment attributes, the results indicated that a declining predictability of economic policies, corruption, high taxes, and financing are negatively associated with investment growth. We also find that the extent of "unofficialdom" (as represented by the extent to which firms underreport their revenues) is significantly associated with macroeconomic instability, tax and regulatory burden, corruption, and inadequate protection of property rights.

Implications

The cross-country enterprise-based data gathered through the WBES and its analysis suggest that survey-based indicators of the business environment can serve as important input to an assessment of a country's business and investment climate. Key variables measured by the WBES that significantly relate to firm-level outcomes point to the importance of assessing the constraints to business when identifying reform priorities in different countries. Furthermore, policy analysis can be enhanced by understanding companies' behavioral responses to different constraints—and by understanding their implications. Thus, finding that firms have a greater tendency to underreport revenue when key policy and institutional conditions are weak has important implications for government efforts to mobilize revenue and improve governance. Indeed, constraints to business are found to have a significant macroeconomic cost beyond their direct effect on lower enterprise growth.

This type of business survey paves the way for a deeper understanding of a firm's behavior in shaping the business environment and investment climate. For example, a major finding of the related research on the transition economy version of the WBES (the Business Environment and Enterprise Performance Survey [BEEPS]) is that, contrary to convention, the firm ought not be seen merely as a passive business climate "taker," traditionally viewing government as the primary source of all business constraints. Instead, the in-depth analysis of the forces of "state capture" highlights the extent to which powerful firms play a key role in shaping the policies, laws, and regulations that form the business environment and investment climate—thus transforming them into business climate "makers"—in countries where state capture is prevalent. This finding underscores the importance of viewing both governance and the investment climate within an integrated framework, and it suggests other issues that cross-country survey instruments might investigate in the future.

The complex interaction between firm size and companies' reported severity of constraints that has been found in this work poses a challenge for policymakers who would target interventions to a single type of firm. Although the relationship between firm size and constraint severity was discovered to exist, it is not declining (with the smallest firms facing the most daunting constraints) for all constraints. Instead, for some constraints, medium-size firms showed no difference, and several such firms actually were more constrained. If those findings are validated through further such empirical studies, some implications will emerge. First, it would then be prudent to focus specifically on each constraint and on the ways it affects firms of different sizes because, depending on the constraint, small, medium, or larger firms may be affected most gravely. Second, such results would argue against targeting policies to small (or medium) enterprises based on the notion that those policies are needed to level the playing field.

Another key finding of this work involves the enormous variance in the nature and severity of different types of constraints across countries and regions. It points up the limited value of engaging in global generalizations regarding the severity of a particular constraint. It also suggests the importance of unbundling generic clusters of constraints; for example, regulatory or governance constraints always will exhibit different manifestations and components and their severity and effect will vary across countries—even where, on average, the generic constraint is rated similarly across such countries.

Furthermore, the country-specific data, initial analysis, and findings emerging from the WBES in this report and other empirical work point out the value of monitoring business environment indicators over time. The relationship shown between key WBES indicators and firm-level outcomes suggests that progress in these indicators should be associated with real improvements in enterprise performance over time. Thus, akin to this survey exercise implemented on a large international basis over a limited period of time, it would be highly advisable to repeat the initiative periodically—perhaps every three years.

Implementing the WBES suggests a few lessons. First, given that WBES was a multipartner venture, optimal coordination by all partners on the core instrument and uniform implementation across countries would ensure reliability and comparability across many variables. Second, as the extensive use of country control variables and "perception-bias control" (or "kvetch;" see chapter four) suggest, it is important to account for inherent biases and measurement errors in any enterprise survey of this type. This calls for care in interpreting results and using control variables. Furthermore, in assessing the investment climate, there is a need to complement survey results with other information. Experience with WBES points to the value of complementing perceptual data with greater use of quantitative questions that evaluate constraints in terms of dollar equivalent amounts, time costs, percentages, and so forth, which would facilitate cross-country comparisons and provide a check on more ordinal values and perceptual responses.

Finally, in the next such survey of firms (beginning in 2002 for some regions), it will be important to aim at a larger firm sample size in each country (to lower the measurement error, although the caveats regarding margins of error will continue to apply), and to maintain comparability with the approach taken during the implementation of the 2000 WBES. This is particularly true for economy-wide sampling, replicating key core questions, and using a similar interview methodology to gather information on a firm's response to the institutional and policy framework and its potential influence on the environment. The WBES experience suggests the high value of parallel international enterprise surveys in generating insights into which policies and institutions contribute most to firm-level growth, investment, and employment—all key elements of a strategy for reducing poverty.

1

Background, Approach, and Sampling

Background

How can one assess and compare the environments for doing business in countries around the world? This is a challenge confronted by the World Bank Group (WBG) and other international financial institutions and investors in their private sector development work and their efforts to assess the investment climate. To encourage economic growth and poverty alleviation, it is important to help countries diagnose where their constraints to investment and business operation lie. Surveys provide not only a diagnostic tool but also an important means of generating consensus around a credible, locally derived information source—that of entrepreneurs and managers who deal each day with the institutions, policies, and practices of the local business environment. Surveys also stimulate analysis and action by providing a comparative basis for examining local conditions and costs.

The World Business Environment Survey (WBES) is a major effort by the WBG and partner institutions to implement a standard core enterprise survey to evaluate business conditions in a large, cross-regional set of countries. It took an important step toward unifying earlier fragmented work to assess conditions for private investment in developing and transition countries, as shaped by local economic policy; governance;[10] regulatory, infrastructure, and financial impediments; and services to businesses. The survey applied a roughly uniform methodology and parallel sample parameters in 80 countries and in the West Bank and Gaza (see table 1.1). Results provide a basis for regional comparisons of investment climates and business environment conditions, and permit comparisons of the severity of constraints that affect enterprises according to such characteristics as size or ownership.[11] In general, at least 100 firms were surveyed in each country.

The results are particularly important in the context of economic globalization. Against a backdrop of growing competition and globalization, member countries increasingly are concerned about how conducive their

Table 1.1 Countries Surveyed and Number of WBESs Completed in Each Country

Country	No. of Surveys	Country	No. of Surveys
East Asia		Haiti	103
Cambodia	326	Honduras	100
China	101	Mexico	100
Indonesia	100	Nicaragua	100
Malaysia	100	Panama	100
Philippines	100	Peru	108
Singapore	100	Trinidad and Tobago	101
Thailand	422	Uruguay	100
		Venezuela, R.B. de	100
Eastern Europe and Central Asia			
Albania	165	*Middle East and Africa*	
Armenia	125	Botswana	101
Azerbaijan	128	Cameroon	57
Belarus	125	Côte d'Ivoire	97
Bosnia and Herzegovina	105	Egypt, Arab Rep. of	102
Bulgaria	125	Ethiopia	105
Croatia	127	Ghana	119
Czech Republic	137	Kenya	113
Estonia	132	Madagascar	116
Georgia	129	Malawi	55
Hungary	129	Namibia	95
Kazakhstan	127	Nigeria	93
Kyrgyz Republic	125	Senegal	124
Lithuania	112	South Africa	121
Moldova	125	Tanzania	83
Poland	225	Tunisia	52
Romania	125	Uganda	137
Russia	525	West Bank and Gaza	93
Slovak Republic	129	Zambia	84
Slovenia	125	Zimbabwe	129
Turkey	150		
Ukraine	225	*OECD (Western Europe/ North America)*	
Uzbekistan	125	Canada	101
		France	100
Latin America and the Caribbean		Germany	100
Argentina	100	Italy	100
Belize	50	Portugal	100
Bolivia	100	Spain	104
Brazil	201	Sweden	102
Chile	100	United Kingdom	102
Colombia	101	United States	100
Costa Rica	100		
Dominican Republic	111	*South Asia*	
Ecuador	100	Bangladesh	50
El Salvador	104	India	210
Guatemala	106	Pakistan	103

business environments are to private investment and business development, and about their relative standing regionally or globally. It is unfortunate that very few indicators allow objective measurement and comparison of the business environment, its binding constraints, and the quality and integrity of supportive and regulatory public services. There are no adequate benchmarks of the relative change in constraint severity and the quality of business services over time. The WBES was intended to fill those gaps. Beginning with substantial seed capital from the WBG Innovation Marketplace, the WBES team sought to accomplish the following objectives:

- to provide feedback from enterprises on the state of the private sector in client countries
- to measure the quality of governance and public services, including the extent of corruption
- to provide better information on constraints to private sector growth from the enterprise perspective
- to sensitize governments and donors to the importance of listening to firms and using the information gained to assess policies critically
- to create internationally comparable indicators that can track changes in a business environment over time and thus allow for both competitive assessment and impact assessments of market-oriented reforms
- to stimulate systematic public–private dialogue on business perceptions and the agenda for reform.

WBES was built on a start made in the enterprise survey conducted for the *1997 World Development Report* (World Bank 1997). With varying sample sizes (as low as 15 enterprises in one country) and methodologies (for example, mail, phone, and in-person data gathering), that survey used a standard set of 25 questions in 67 countries. The WBES used many of the same questions but substantially broadened coverage on a number of issues, expanded the sample and the number of countries covered, and harmonized methodologies across countries by using only direct interviews (except in Africa where mail surveys predominated).[12]

Survey Approach

Before the WBES was created, consistent firm-level data to analyze business constraints to efficient operation and growth were not available for many countries. (See the annex to this chapter for a summary of emerging best-practice lessons about the design and use of enterprise surveys.) The WBES[13] steering committee, in an effort to generate the desired data from a representative sample of firms in the manufacturing and services sectors of each geographic region studied, developed a core survey instrument.

The team collaborated with its partners in different regions and countries to implement the survey and to develop regional modules that would capture in detail issues considered important to those regions. This book, however, focuses on the findings from the common core questionnaire. The survey instrument (annex 1 at the back of the book) is broad in its coverage and includes a wealth of information on firm and business environment attributes. Firm-level attributes include firm size (number of employees, amount of sales, and assets); years of operation; sales, debt, and growth performance (trends); sources of finance; and a mix of qualitative and quantitative evaluations of such business environment features as corruption and governance, the regulatory regime, economic policy predictability, the nature of competition, public service delivery, the judicial system, financing, and general constraints to operations.

The design of the sampling frame reflected several considerations. In general, the sample aimed to reflect the relative importance of manufacturing firms versus service and commercial firms in the economy. To ensure representative findings across countries, a sample frame was developed for most countries to reflect the distribution of privately owned companies in each country by sector, size (measured by number of employees), and location. In most developing and transition countries, commercially available databases are inadequate.[14] Each consulting firm hired to conduct regional surveys used desk research to generate a suitable sample frame, the primary research source being government registers of enterprises that are maintained by most of the countries under review.

To ensure adequate representation of firms by industry, size, ownership, export orientation, and location, the following sampling targets were agreed on across all regions:

- *Sectoral composition:* The numbers of manufacturing versus service companies were allocated according to their contribution to gross domestic product (GDP), with a 15 percent minimum for each type of firm.
- *Size:* At least 15 percent of the sample was in the small category (fewer than 50 employees) and at least 15 percent was in the large category (more than 500 employees).
- *Ownership:* At least 15 percent of the companies in the sample were firms with foreign control (where the law prohibited such a control arrangement, the companies had substantial foreign ownership).
- *Exporters:* At least 15 percent of firms exported at least 20 percent of their output.
- *Location:* At least 15 percent of firms were located in small towns (a population of less than 50,000), or in the countryside.

The survey was implemented by the Gallup Organization in East Asia, Pakistan, Latin America, and countries in the Organisation for Economic

Co-operation and Development (OECD); by AC Nielsen in Eastern Europe and Turkey; by the Confederation of Indian Industries in India; by the Harvard Center for International Development in Africa; by the Egyptian Center for Economic Studies in Egypt; by LIDEE Khmer in Cambodia; by the University of the Chamber of Commerce in Thailand; and by the Bangladesh export development project in Bangladesh.

Surveys were conducted over a period of roughly 20 months between the end of 1998 and the middle of 2000. Data were collected though personal interviews conducted with enterprise managers in most regions, and predominantly by mail in Africa. Response rates generally were high, except for responses to questions on corruption. By region, response rates were among the lowest in Africa. All of the analyses in this report are based on a sample of 10,090 enterprises that responded to the core questionnaire. The sample distribution, by country, generally met the minimum goal of 100 firms (see table 1.1).

Actual Characteristics of the Sample

Table 1.2 presents the sample organized by country income. Using the classifications of the *World Development Report 2000,* a third of the countries are categorized as low income (per capita income of U.S.$760 or less); roughly half are middle-income countries (per capita income of U.S.$761–$9,360), and slightly less than a fifth of the sample are high-income countries (per capita income more than U.S.$9,360). These differences across economies are an important source of variation in the business environment in which local firms operate and they influence firm performance. Another important source of variation is the differences that exist within each country, and across firms of different sizes, activities, and other characteristics. Both sources of variation are studied in this report to highlight the key constraints facing businesses and their potential effects on growth and performance.

Table 1.3 presents the regional breakdown of firms by size and business category. Both small and medium enterprises (SMEs; those with 500 or fewer workers) and large firms (those with 501 or more employees) were sampled in the WBES. As shown in table 1.3, the clear majority of samples (80 percent) were SMEs, with an almost equal proportion of small enterprises (50 or fewer employees) and medium enterprises (51–500 employees). Large firms accounted for about 20 percent of the sample.

The sample's differences in industry categories generally reflect the variations within national economies. Of firms that could be classified, the most common activity was the services/commerce category, which accounted for 43 percent of all firms interviewed, followed by manufacturing (36 percent), construction (9 percent), agriculture (7 percent),[15] and "other" (4.3 percent).

Table 1.2 WBES Countries, Territory by Income

Low Income	Middle Income		High Income
Armenia	Albania	Lithuania	Bosnia
Azerbaijan	Argentina	Malaysia	Canada
Bangladesh	Belarus	Mexico	France
Cambodia	Belize	Namibia	Germany
Cameroon	Bolivia	Panama	Italy
China	Botswana	Peru	Portugal
Côte d'Ivoire	Brazil	Philippines	Singapore
Ethiopia	Bulgaria	Poland	Slovenia
Ghana	Chile	Romania	Spain
Haiti	Colombia	Russia	Sweden
Honduras	Costa Rica	Slovak Republic	United Kingdom
India	Croatia	South Africa	United States
Indonesia	Czech Rep.	Thailand	
Kenya	Dominican Rep.	Trinidad and	
Kyrgyz Republic	Ecuador	Tobago	
Madagascar	Egypt, Arab	Tunisia	
Malawi	Rep. of	Turkey	
Moldova	El Salvador	Ukraine	
Nicaragua	Estonia	Uruguay	
Nigeria	Georgia	Uzbekistan	
Pakistan	Guatemala	Venezuela, R.B. de	
Senegal	Hungary	West Bank and	
Tanzania	Kazakhstan	Gaza	
Uganda			
Zambia			
Zimbabwe			

Table 1.3 Distribution of Surveyed Firms by Region, Size, and Main Activity*

	Manufacturing	Services/ commerce	Agriculture	Construction	Other/ multiple	Total firms
Africa						
Small	16.7	28.9	5.7	24.2	24.4	508
Medium	30.1	26.8	8.0	16.3	18.8	485
Large	36.6	25.4	8.7	14.0	15.4	358
Total	26.8	27.2	7.3	18.7	20.0	1,351
CEE						
Small	21.9	60.6	7.2	9.9	0.4	718
Medium	29.2	27.7	30.2	12.9	0.1	902
Large	54.3	12.4	28.7	4.7	0	129
Total	28.0	40.1	20.6	11.0	0.2	1,749

(continued on next page)

Table 1.3, *continued*

	Manufacturing	Services/ commerce	Agriculture	Construction	Other/ multiple	Total firms
CIS						
Small	20.8	63.5	4.4	8.2	3.1	903
Medium	49.3	34.7	5.7	6.6	3.7	683
Large	60.3	27.0	6.3	5.2	1.1	174
Total	35.8	48.7	5.1	7.3	3.1	1,760
East Asia Developing						
Small	36.4	54.5	3.5	5.6	0	536
Medium	48.7	45.5	1.1	4.7	0	279
Large	68.8	28.1	3.1	0	0	128
Total	44.4	48.3	2.8	4.6	0	943
East Asia NIC/China						
Small	41.0	49.3	1.5	8.2	0	134
Medium	55.1	37.1	1.1	6.7	0	89
Large	53.8	38.5	0	7.7	0	78
Total	48.5	42.9	1.0	7.6	0	301
LAC						
Small	36.4	53.6	2.0	8.1	0	459
Medium	45.1	47.1	1.5	6.3	0	669
Large	53.4	38.5	3.5	4.6	0	481
Total	45.1	46.4	2.2	6.3	0	1,609
MENA						
Small	60.0	20.0	0	8.9	11.1	45
Medium	31.6	35.5	6.6	7.9	18.4	76
Large	31.0	41.4	8.6	8.6	10.3	58
Total	38.5	33.5	5.6	8.4	14.0	246
OECD						
Small	21.7	64.5	1.3	12.6	0	318
Medium	30.3	60.2	1.0	8.2	0	389
Large	33.5	63.5	0.6	2.4	0	167
Total	27.8	62.4	1.0	8.7	0	874
South Asia						
Small	43.2	39.5	1.2	4.9	11.1	81
Medium	64.1	20.0	1.8	1.8	12.4	171
Large	82.6	9.2	0	1.8	6.4	111
Total	65.0	21.1	1.1	2.5	10.3	363

Total = regional average.
*Table omits firms that could not be classified by main activity and size due to missing information.

Consistent with regional sector contributions to GDP, Eastern Europe and the OECD had a higher proportion of firms in the services sector, whereas South Asia had the highest proportion of firms in manufacturing. SMEs also are consistently less involved in manufacturing than are large firms and more involved in services and commerce. Differences in administration of the survey in Sub-Saharan and North Africa led to a large category of firms that could not be placed in one of the four main business categories.

The findings reported here are an accurate representation of the study sample in light of the objectives of the WBES. However, there is one important caveat on all results reported in this book: they are unweighted. Given that certain subgroups, including large firms, generally were oversampled, being unweighted has two implications. First, the views of enterprises in small countries in each region carry the same importance as those of the major countries in the region (unless the sample size in those countries happened to be larger). Second, the findings are somewhat skewed toward the larger enterprises in each country. Thus, the caution at the outset of this report remains: Given inherent error margins arising from small samples that are drawn in a targeted manner, individual indicators should not be used for precise country rankings in any particular dimension of the investment climate or governance.

Table 1.4 shows the main attributes of firms surveyed by region. On average, roughly a third of the firms are export oriented, with an average export-to-sales ratio among exporters of 38 percent. Firms in Africa, the Middle East and North Africa (MENA), and South Asia have a higher percentage of exporting firms, which account for almost half of the sample; in sharp contrast, the percentage of exporting firms is lowest in Central and Eastern European countries (CEE) at 15 percent. However, the intensity of exports is highest in East Asian (developing) nations, where the average export-to-sales ratio is 64 percent and sharply higher than the other regions.

Firm ownership is mainly domestic and private. Twelve percent of firms reported having some state ownership. By region, state ownership ranges from 20 percent in countries of the Commonwealth of Independent States (CIS) and in CEE countries (this was part of the sample design agreed to with the European Bank for Reconstruction and Development (EBRD), to 2 percent in East Asia (developing) and 3 percent in Latin America and the Caribbean. By activity, 23 percent of firms in the WBES sample engaged in manufacturing, 18 percent in agriculture, and only 5 percent in commerce reported some degree of state ownership. In firms reporting a degree of state ownership, the extent of such ownership was, on average, about 70 percent. Nineteen percent of firms in the sample reported having some amount of foreign ownership. Among that subset, the average foreign share of capital was 67 percent. The samples in Sub-

Table 1.4 Trade, Ownership, and Age Characteristics of Companies Surveyed, by Region and Regional Group

Region or regional group	Exporting firms (% of firms)	If exporter, percentage of total sales exported	Percentage of firms with foreign ownership	If foreign owned, percentage of foreign ownership	Percentage of firms with state ownership	If state owned, percentage of state ownership	Average age of firm
Africa	52	34.0	30	80.8	10	91.2	a
CEE	15	29.1	5	48.1	22	67.7	9.5
CIS	42	36.3	11	58.2	24	67.5	15.4
East Asia Developing	32	64.3	25	70.3	2	60.1	12.7
East Asia NIC/China	40	49.8	30	67.1	11	76.4	16.2
LAC	33	37.9	23	69.8	3	56.0	24.9
MENA[b]	51	42.5	13	60.5	11	72.9	a
OECD	37	28.8	23	61.0	8	55.3	34.1
South Asia	55	33.7	24	32.2	11	31.2	22.3
Total	36	37.9	19	66.8	12	68.3	18.7

a. Exact ages of firms in Africa are not available. Instead, firms were grouped in three age categories: less than 5 years—20 percent; 5–15 years—29 percent; more than 15 years—51 percent.
b. Exact ages of firms in MENA are not available. Instead, firms were grouped in three age categories: less than 5 years—13 percent; 5–15 years—39 percent; more than 15 years—48 percent.

Saharan Africa and East Asia NIC/China have the highest percentage of firms with foreign ownership (30 percent) and Africa and developing East Asia the highest share of foreign capital among foreign-owned firms. South Asian firms had the lowest percentage of foreign ownership, with foreign capital investment at 32 percent.

In terms of firm age, on average the youngest firms were for those in Central and Eastern Europe (9.5 years). The oldest average company age was in OECD nations (34.1 years).

The most common legal organization of firms interviewed was the privately held corporation, which accounts for an average of close to one-third of all enterprises in each region (table 1.5). This form was especially prevalent in the samples in Africa, MENA, China, and the newly industrialized nations of East Asia. In Latin America, other (unspecified) forms of organization and partnerships predominate. Sole proprietorships were the second most common form of organization, representing a fifth of the enterprises surveyed and accounting for a third of the enterprises in developing East Asia, but only 10 percent of enterprises in Africa. Partnerships accounted for 18 percent of enterprises overall, including 28 percent of firms interviewed in MENA. Cooperatives were relatively uncommon, accounting for only 3 percent of those interviewed, and were most prevalent in CEE countries (11 percent).[16]

Table 1.5 Legal Form of Companies Surveyed, by Region and Regional Group (Percentage of Firms, by Category)

Region or regional group	Sole proprietorship	Partnership	Cooperative	Corporation, privately held	Corporation listed on stock exchange	Other
Africa	10	11	1	45	12	21
CEE	23	20	11	26	19	1
CIS	33	24	2	27	7	6
East Asia Developing	36	18	1	39	4	1
East Asia NIC/China	12	11	5	48	7	16
LAC	15	23	1	17	4	40
MENA	12	28	5	41	9	5
OECD	12	12	2	36	14	24
South Asia	12	12	1	35	30	9
Total	20	18	3	31	10	17

Total = average for all firms in the WBES sample.

Table 1.6 Operations in Other Countries and Sales to the Public Sector among Companies Surveyed

Region or regional group	Percentage of firms with operations in other countries	Percentage of firms with sales to public sector	Percentage of sales to public sector
Africa	32	60	n.a.
CEE	3	55	37
CIS	12	52	27
East Asia NIC/China	28	27	41
East Asia Developing	15	38	24
LAC	25	47	18
MENA	19	n.a.	n.a.
OECD	25	42	23
South Asia[a]	18	60	22
Total	18	50	24

n.a. Not asked.
a. India is not included in category for percentage of firms with sales to public sector and percentage of sales to public sector.
Total = average for all firms in the WBES sample.

As shown by region in Table 1.6, an average of 18 percent of the firms surveyed have holdings or operations in other countries. The highest incidence is found in Africa (32 percent);[17] by contrast, developing countries in East Asia (15 percent), CIS (12 percent), and CEE (3 percent) are well below the sample average, with a higher proportion of firms operating almost exclusively within their own country borders.

About half of all firms surveyed trade with the public sector (table 1.6). The substantial variation by region and country reflects the varying economic power of the state and the nature of the firms surveyed within countries in a region. The proportion of firms selling to the public sector is highest in South Asia (60 percent) and Africa (60 percent). Although the lowest incidence is in East Asian newly industrialized countries (27 percent), the proportion of sales to the state sector is highest in that region (41 percent). On average, the public sector represents 24 percent of sales to those firms trading with it. The proportion is lowest in MENA (13 percent) and LAC (18 percent).

Annex:
Emerging Lessons on the Design and Use of Surveys

Survey Value

Listening to the problems of active entrepreneurs is an important step toward identifying needed reforms in the business environment. Survey data can illuminate: respondents' priorities for reform, the private costs imposed by business environment constraints, and the functioning of policies "on the ground" in a country's unique institutional setting. Uniform questionnaires uniformly administered may be compared across countries to better evaluate responses using international benchmarks, and may facilitate the tracking of reform progress over time. To attain useful results, however, care must be taken in the design of a questionnaire, the selection of a sample, the administration of the survey, and the analysis and interpretation of the results. Although surveys can be performed economically, they must not be shortchanged on planning and care in implementation. It is equally important that survey results be kept in perspective, always balanced with other information sources and with common sense.

Sample Design

Most surveys to date have relied on some form of stratified random sampling. Strata have been chosen either broadly to represent the entire economy (for example, by sector, location, size, or any combination of the three), or more narrowly to investigate priority areas of the economy (for example, the manufacturing sector), or to highlight phenomena of special interest (for example, productivity in particular sectors, industries with long contracting horizons, and the like). Across or within selected strata, a list of industries is acquired to constitute the sample frame. Then a random, structured, or stratified selection method is employed. In cases where available lists are known to have systematic biases (or where firms having desired characteristics [such as foreign ownership] are rare in the general population), oversampling, nonrandom methods (such as quota sampling), or area-based methods have been used to improve representation.

Questionnaire Design

The WBG relies on standardized core questions used in multiple countries to represent the experience and perceptions of businesses in comparable ways across countries and over time. The use of core groups of

Adapted from Stone 2002.

questions in surveys is beginning to allow international comparisons of the severity and costs imposed by different factors in the investment climate. For valid comparisons to be drawn, sample design must also be standardized.

Business environment enterprise surveys generally have been performed under strict time and budgetary constraints. The instrument itself has been kept short so that it can be completed in a single one- to two-hour session with the senior manager (sometimes supplemented by a session with the firm's accountant or human resources director), and to ensure that randomly selected entrepreneurs would respond to the entire questionnaire. To achieve this brevity, surveys have been forced to trade between breadth and depth.

Questionnaires usually are divided into sections, beginning with simple (and "safe") background information and moving to a series of substantive areas of the designer's choosing, such as "regulation," "finance," and "infrastructure." A typical sequence of questions would move from the general to the specific to the comparative. A critical concern with surveys has been to evaluate cost—particularly the burden imposed on businesses by the fiscal and regulatory environment and by inadequate public infrastructure, financial systems, and other services. Surveys initially focused on relative costs, using ranked responses. Such methodology rests on the hypothesis that the constraint rankings assigned by firms reflect the (unobserved) incremental costs associated with the constraints. Therefore, constraint scores reveal the ranking of the shadow prices for different constraints. Such rankings allow comparisons and enable investigators to determine the enterprise characteristics associated with high and low constraint scores, as well as to identify the collective business perspective on priorities for reform. For example, the WBES instrument is based on a nested structure of constraint and qualitative rankings, with a general constraint question and specific sets of questions on regulatory constraints, financial constraints, quality of public services, and so forth. Ranking alone, however, does not provide a monetary equivalent to the constraint score.

Increasingly, surveys have also focused on obtaining quantitative estimates of costs. Direct estimates of cost prove particularly useful when analyzing regulatory burden and other costs that involve discrete payments or expenditures of time by the firm. Direct questions probe expenditures of money or time on particular activities or items, such as the cost of business licenses or the monthly operating cost of a generator to compensate for poor public power supply. Questions also may concern days of business lost, for example, to inspections, power interruptions, or strikes. Indirect questions try to get entrepreneurs to assign values to things that have no well-defined monetary or labor costs. Contingent valuation questions ask entrepreneurs what percent of gross sales they would sacrifice to be free from particular constraints.

Survey Implementation

Before launching the survey, the questionnaire itself must be tested to ensure that the questions are comprehensible to respondents, that the responses elicit the desired information, that none of the questions seriously offends or threatens respondents, and that the entire survey does not take too long. There always will be problems or opportunities to improve questions and opportunities to adjust language and questions to suit local usage and local institutions—something that will increase respondents' enthusiasm. Survey costs vary substantially depending on a number of conditions, including the length and design of the survey itself, the number of firms to be included, the number of different economic sectors examined, and the number and dispersion of locations at which the survey will be administered. Cost also depends on who administers the survey.

In selecting a local consultant to administer the survey, the following factors are critical to success:

- experience carrying out enterprise surveys or, second best, public opinion or market research surveys
- knowledge of business issues from entrepreneurial and policy perspectives
- access to sources of information on firms required to construct the sample frame
- access to firms
- ability to mobilize, train, and supervise qualified surveyors (enumerators)
- ability to control quality in survey implementation, data entry, and analysis
- ability to analyze or assist in analyzing results both quantitatively and qualitatively.

Even with experienced local consultants conducting the survey work, proper orientation and training are key. Very few people have administered a World Bank private enterprise survey so the types of questions being asked and even the subject of the survey may be unfamiliar to potential surveyors. Orient them to the purpose of the survey, the etiquette of interviewing, the importance of confidentiality, and the correct method for recording and encoding data. It is useful to illustrate the value of surveys with examples from past Bank work. Adequate quality control of survey forms and data entry will avoid large losses of data arising from entry errors, unreadable responses, or incomplete or inaccurate forms.

Using Results

Properly designed surveys have a distinct legitimacy with local businesses and policymakers, so they make excellent focal points for policy and project consultations. To make survey results useful to clients and to country strategy and operations, surveys should be followed up by direct consultation of both government counterparts and the private sector on priority issues and implications identified by the survey.

2

Business Environment Constraints

Leading Constraints on Business Operation and Growth

The survey asked respondents to rate how problematic a set of general constraints were for the growth and operation of their firms. Table 2.1 presents the ranking of responses for the world, by regional groups, and by individual region to the question: "Please judge on a four-point scale how problematic are the following factors for the operation and growth of your firm." Looking at a simple average for the world sample, four constraints stand out as "major" or "moderate": taxes and regulations, financing, policy uncertainty/instability, and inflation.

Yet such worldwide averages mask crucial differences across regions, particularly between industrialized and developing countries. For nations in the Organisation for Economic Co-operation and Development (OECD), newly industrialized East Asian countries, and transition economies, the leading obstacles identified by the firms were taxes and regulations, financing, policy instability, and inflation. However, when the answers were averaged for developing regions (the countries of Africa; Latin America and the Caribbean [LAC]; Middle East and North Africa [MENA]; South Asia; and developing East Asia), the leading constraint was corruption, followed by inflation, financing, policy instability, and infrastructure. Indeed, in four developing regions—South Asia, Africa, East Asia, and MENA—corruption was one of the three leading constraints.

There are also significant differences among individual regions in the severity of constraints. This large variance points to the importance of assessing the results by region and country, rather than relying on worldwide averages. Consequently, the following section concentrates on more detailed regional patterns.

- In *Africa* (where the constraints of the judicial system and anticompetitive practices were not evaluated), infrastructure emerged as one of the

Table 2.1 General Constraints on Firms

	Leading constraint	Second constraint	Third constraint	Fourth constraint
World	Taxes and regulations	Financing	Policy instability	Inflation
Regional Groups				
OECD and Newly Industrial East Asia countries (NIC East Asia, including China)	Taxes and regulations	Financing	Policy instability	Inflation
Transition Europe (Central Europe and former Soviet Union members [CIS])	Taxes and regulations	Financing	Inflation	Policy instability
Developing countries (Africa, Middle East and North Africa [MENA], East Asia Developing, South Asia, Latin America and the Caribbean [LAC])	Corruption	Inflation	Financing	Policy instability / infrastructure (tie)
Regions				
Africa	Financing	Corruption	Infrastructure	Inflation
MENA	Policy instability	Corruption	Inflation	Exchange rate
NIC East Asia	Financing	Inflation	Anticompetitive practices	Policy instability
East Asia Developing	Street crime	Corruption	Inflation/exchange rate/organized crime (tie)	
South Asia	Corruption/policy instability (tie)	Policy instability	Inflation	Infrastructure
LAC	Taxes and regulations	Financing	Street crime	Financing
OECD	Taxes and regulations	Financing	Policy instability	Inflation
Commonwealth of Independent States (CIS) [former Soviet Union members]	Taxes and regulations	Financing	Policy instability	Inflation
Central and Eastern Europe (CEE) [non-CIS]	Taxes and regulations/inflation (tie)		Financing	Policy instability

most important constraints, along with financing, corruption, and inflation (see figure 2.1). Each was evaluated by 60 percent or more of firms as moderate or major constraints.

- In *Central and Eastern Europe,* taxes and regulations and inflation were judged to be the leading constraints; each was evaluated by at least 80 percent of firms as moderate or major (see figure 2.2). At least 70 percent of firms identified financing, policy uncertainty/instability, and the exchange rate as serious constraints.
- For the *Commonwealth of Independent States* (former Soviet Union members), taxes and regulations led all other constraints, identified by more than three-quarters of firms as serious (see figure 2.3). Financing and policy instability were serious constraints for at least 60 percent of firms, and inflation followed close behind.
- *Developing East Asian* countries stood out in having the highest number of constraints identified as moderate or major by more than half the firms—10 of 11 (see figure 2.4). The leading constraints were street crime and policy instability, each identified by more than 70 percent of firms as serious. More than 60 percent of firms found corruption, organized crime, inflation, and the exchange rate to be serious constraints.
- In *newly industrial Asia and China,* only financing was identified by more than half of the firms as a moderate or major constraint (see figure 2.5). No more than 31 percent of firms identified any other constraint (inflation) as serious.

Figure 2.1 General Constraints on Firms: Countries in Africa

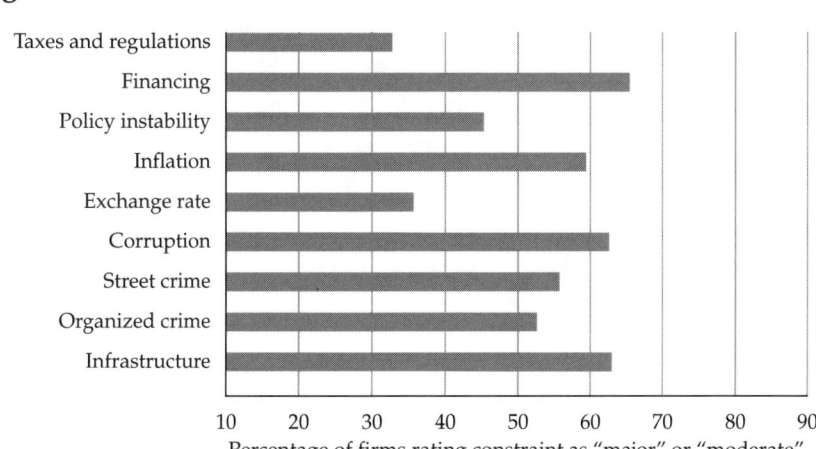

Percentage of firms rating constraint as "major" or "moderate"

- In *Latin America,* more than 70 percent of firms identified taxes and regulations and policy uncertainty/instability as serious concerns, whereas more than 60 percent found street crime, financing, inflation, and

**Figure 2.2 General Constraints on Firms: Countries in
Central and Eastern Europe (Non-CIS)**

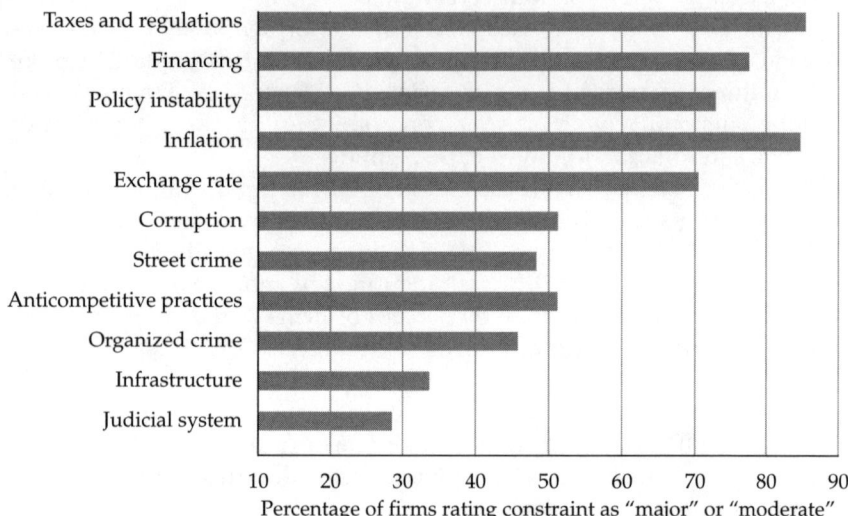

Percentage of firms rating constraint as "major" or "moderate"

Figure 2.3 General Constraints on Firms: CIS Countries

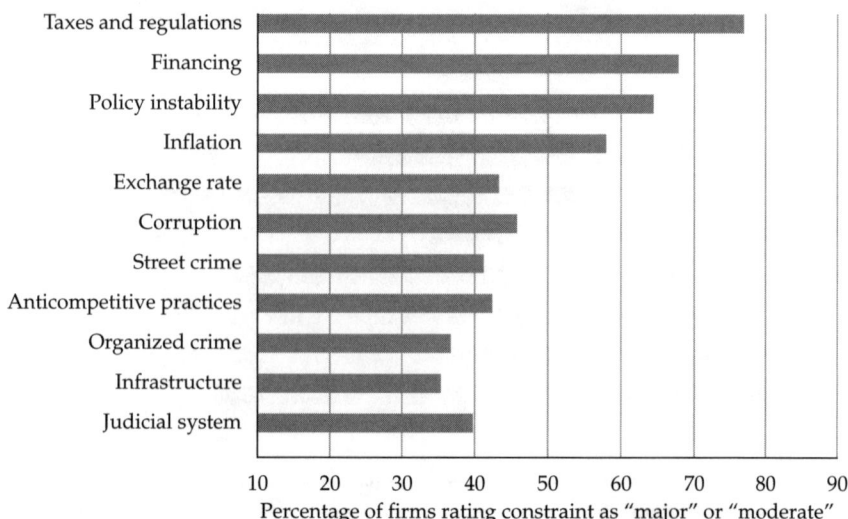

Percentage of firms rating constraint as "major" or "moderate"

the exchange rate to be moderate or major constraints (see figure 2.6). Nearly 60 percent found corruption a serious constraint.

Figure 2.4 General Constraints on Firms: Countries in East Asia (Developing)

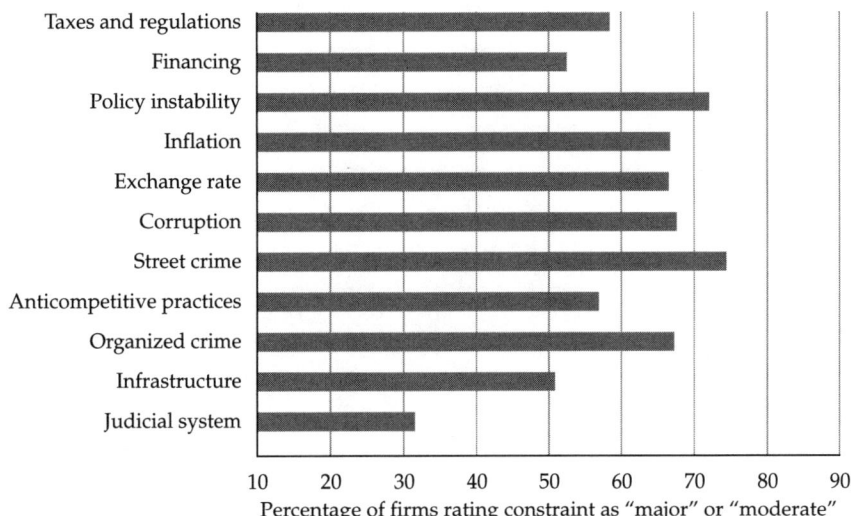

Percentage of firms rating constraint as "major" or "moderate"

Figure 2.5 General Constraints on Firms: Countries in East Asia (NIC and China)

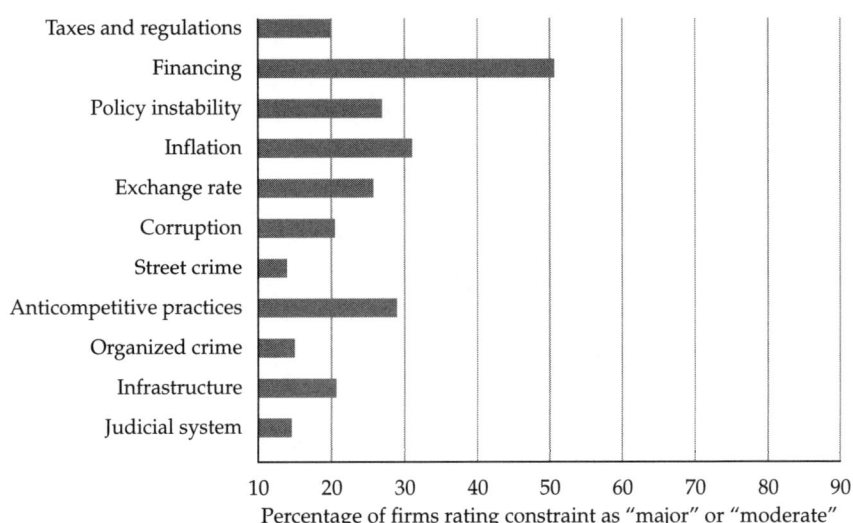

Percentage of firms rating constraint as "major" or "moderate"

Figure 2.6 General Constraints on Firms: LAC Countries

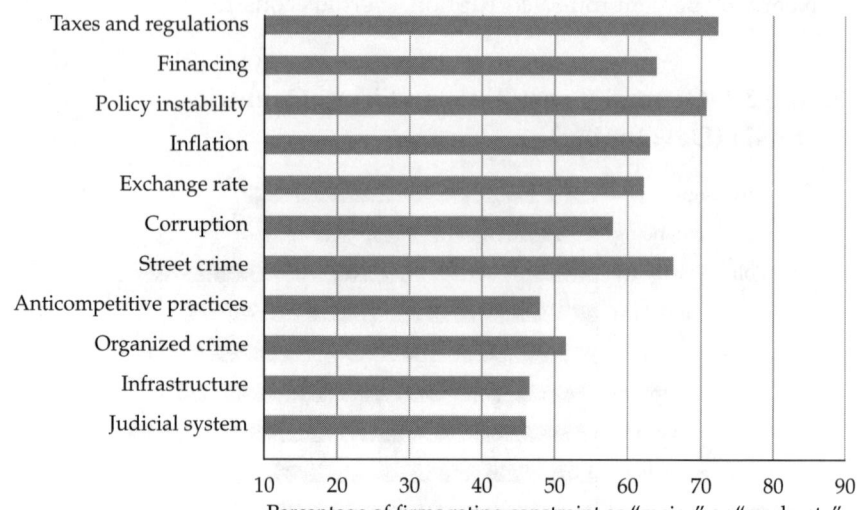

Percentage of firms rating constraint as "major" or "moderate"

- In the *Middle East/North Africa* region, more than 65 percent of surveyed firms found policy uncertainty/instability and corruption to be serious constraints (see figure 2.7). More than half the firms identified taxes and regulations, inflation, the exchange rate, and anticompetitive practices as moderate or major constraints.
- Firms in *OECD* nations identified only one leading constraint—taxes and regulations—which was singled out by more than 60 percent of firms (see figure 2.8). No more than 40 percent of firms identified any other constraint as moderate or major, although nearly 40 percent of the firms rated financing as a major or moderate constraint.
- In *South Asia,* policy uncertainty/instability and corruption led all other constraints, and were identified by 72 percent of firms as serious constraints (see figure 2.9). More than 60 percent of firms identified financing, inflation, and infrastructure as serious constraints.

Small and medium-size enterprises (SMEs) identified themselves as more constrained by most categories of obstacles than did large firms (see figure 2.10). A substantially higher percentage of SMEs rated the top two overall constraints, taxes and regulations and financing, as serious constraints than did large enterprises. Large differences also existed in perceptions of the importance of inflation and anticompetitive practices by other businesses or government, with a substantially smaller percentage of large firms identifying themselves as seriously constrained by these factors. For a subset of rule of law issues—corruption, street crime, and organized crime—small firms held themselves to be more constrained

Figure 2.7 General Constraints on Firms: MENA Countries

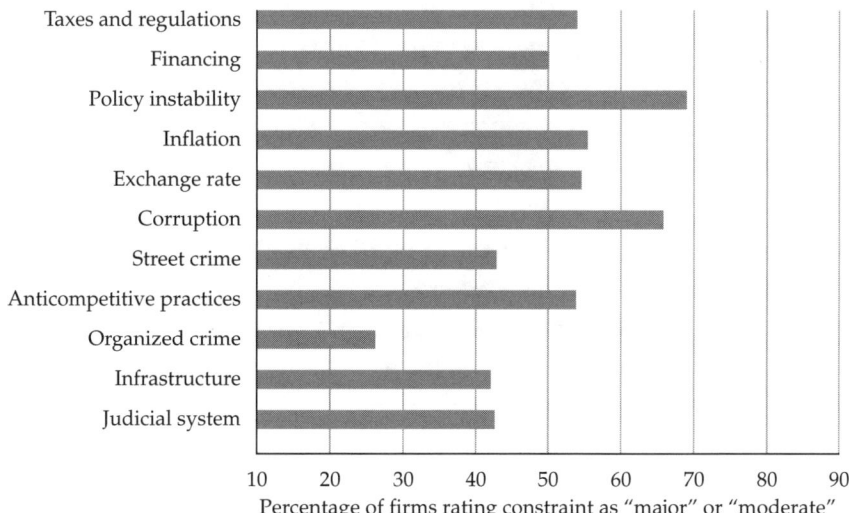

Percentage of firms rating constraint as "major" or "moderate"

Figure 2.8 General Constraints on Firms: OECD Countries

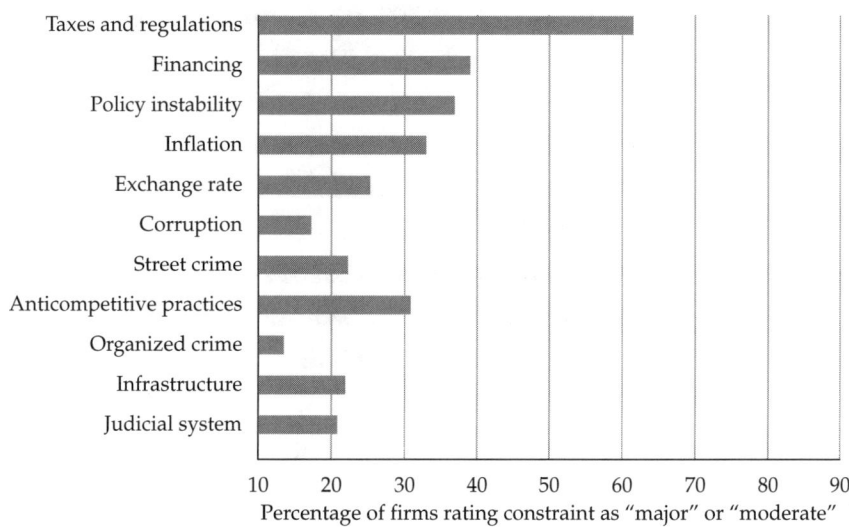

Percentage of firms rating constraint as "major" or "moderate"

than did medium-size and large firms. Only in infrastructure were large firms significantly more constrained in terms of the percentage of firms identifying this constraint as moderate or major.

Figure 2.9 General Constraints on Firms: Countries in South Asia

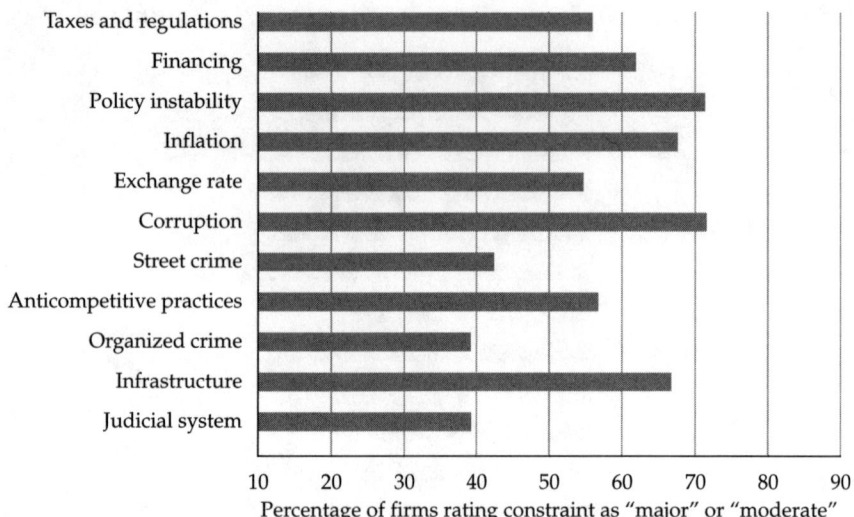

Percentage of firms rating constraint as "major" or "moderate"

Figure 2.10 General Constraints on Firms, by Size of Firm

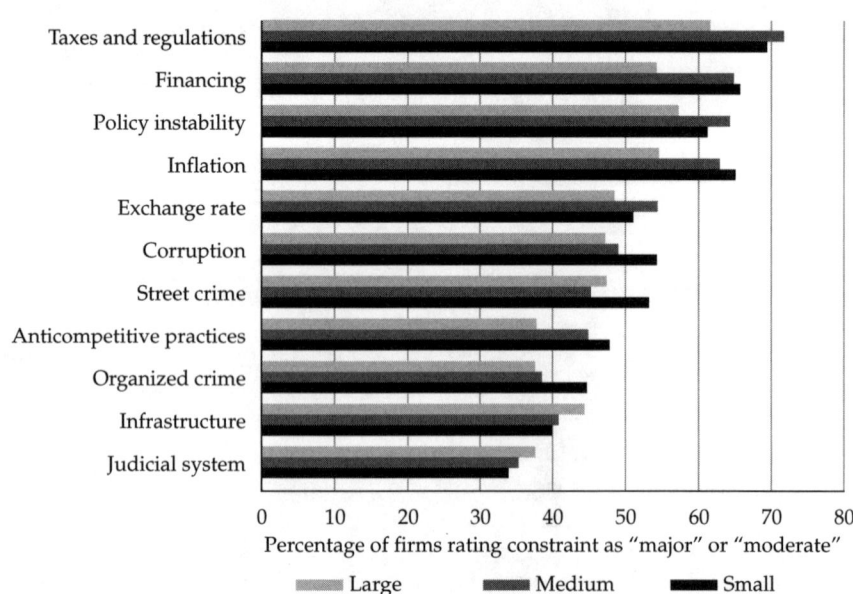

Percentage of firms rating constraint as "major" or "moderate"

Box 2.1 Do Perceptions Differ among Foreign-Owned Firms?

Do firms with foreign capital perceive constraints differently from domestic firms? An analysis of average constraint scores (Nagarajan and others 2001) suggests that on a global scale, foreign-owned and joint-venture firms identify themselves as less severely constrained than do domestically owned firms, except with regard to infrastructure, for which foreign firms identify themselves as more constrained. However, many of these differences by ownership do not hold within regions. The main exception is financing, in which in every region firms with foreign capital identified themselves as less constrained. However, the regression analysis presented in chapter four suggests that most of these apparent differences in firm experience can be attributed to firm characteristics other than ownership.

Major Constraints in Detail

The following sections examine the responses for each category of constraint by region and firm size. In selected cases, we also note differences between foreign and domestically financed firms (see box 2.1). Each section then describes responses to detailed questions on that category of constraint.

Taxes and Regulations

Inappropriately designed or administered tax and regulatory systems can substantially reduce a firm's ability to compete internationally, distort investment decisions, or deter investment entirely. Taxes and regulations are an important source of both direct and indirect costs for firms. Firms may identify regulations as burdensome for a variety of reasons: they may impose direct costs (for example, formal and informal payments, facilitation costs, expenditures of staff time) or indirect costs (for example, the inefficient allocation of firm resources in response to the incentives created by regulation and regulatory enforcement).

Figure 2.11 shows that a higher percentage of firms in the transitional economies of Central Europe and CIS found taxes and regulations to be a serious (major or moderate) constraint. Close behind are firms in the Latin America and Caribbean region. In most other regions, more than half the firms also found this category to be a serious constraint.

Conversely, only 4 in 10 firms surveyed in Africa found this to be a serious general constraint, and in the newly industrialized countries of East Asia (including China), only 20 percent found this category to be a serious constraint. As already noted, although the taxes and regulations category posed the leading constraint category for firms in each size group, a statistically significant lower percentage of large firms found it a moderate or major constraint (see figure 2.12).

Figure 2.11 Taxes and Regulations, by Region and Regional Group

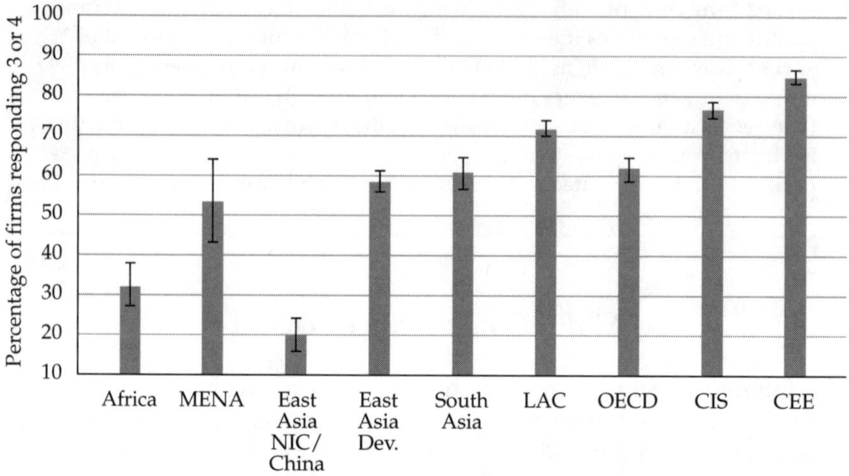

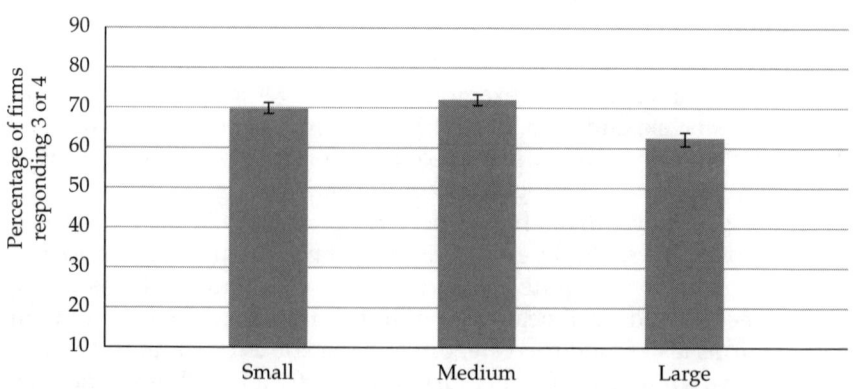

Notes: Error bars represent 95 percent confidence interval. Response options were: 1 = no obstacle; 2 = minor obstacle; 3 = moderate obstacle; 4 = major obstacle.

Figure 2.12 Taxes and Regulations, by Size of Firm

Notes: Error bars represent 95 percent confidence interval. Response options were: 1 = no obstacle; 2 = minor obstacle; 3 = moderate obstacle; 4 = major obstacle.

WBES provides a measure of one key dimension of regulatory compliance cost: the cost of regulatory compliance through time spent by senior managers who must work with government officials on the application and interpretation of laws and regulations. As figure 2.13 shows, firms in South Asia and developing East Asia had the highest costs, with an average of approximately 15 percent of senior management time spent dealing with public officials. Central and Eastern European firms rated themselves close behind, with an average of 14 percent. Firms in MENA lost more than 12 percent of their time to officials. For African firms, this figure was 12 percent. Firms in CIS countries claimed to spend only about 8 percent of their time working with officials, firms in the newly industrialized countries of East Asia spent 6 percent of their time doing so, firms in OECD countries spent more than 5 percent of their time doing so, and firms in the Latin America and Caribbean region (the least burdened in this regard) still spent more than 4 percent of their time doing so. Time lost to regulatory compliance means firms in poor investment climates must either operate with 10 percent less management time or it may mean that larger firms must hire more managers.

Regulatory quality also can be evaluated in other terms, including the transparency and predictability of rules and the fairness and consistency

Figure 2.13 Percentage of Management Time Spent Dealing with Government Officials Concerning Application and Interpretation of Laws

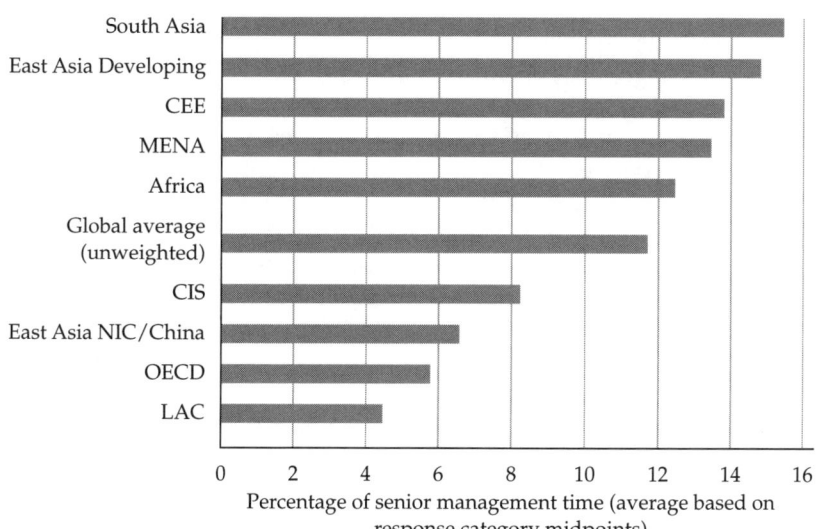

Percentage of senior management time (average based on response category midpoints)

Figure 2.14 Business Registration Regulations, by Region and Regional Group

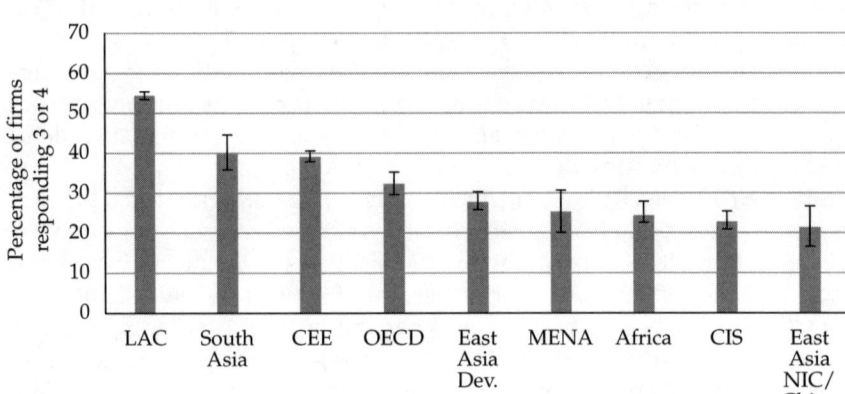

Notes: Error bars represent 95 percent confidence interval. Response options were: 1 = no obstacle; 2 = minor obstacle; 3 = moderate obstacle; 4 = major obstacle.

of their implementation. Firms rated the predictability of policies and the laws and regulations affecting them on a six-point scale ranging from "completely predictable" to "completely unpredictable." The majority of firms in seven of nine regions said that laws and regulations were somewhat unpredictable, whereas in African, CEE, and CIS nations at least two-thirds of firms said that laws and regulations were unpredictable (these results are elaborated later in the section on policy instability and uncertainty).

The WBES asked firms to evaluate the severity of a list of potential regulatory constraints. As table 2.2 shows, *high taxes* topped this list in every region. Because taxes are generally an unavoidable and significant cost of doing business, it is not surprising that most businesses believe that taxes are too high. Firms in LAC, CEE, and CIS countries were most likely to feel constrained; between 80 percent and 90 percent of firms in each region found that high taxes were a serious constraint. In African, East Asian developing, South Asian, and OECD nations, more than 70 percent of firms found that high taxes were a serious constraint, whereas a slight majority of firms in MENA countries agreed. It is noteworthy that the majority of firms in newly industrialized East Asia did not identify high taxes as a serious constraint, and more generally, said they were not seriously constrained by any category of regulation.

Independent of the direct cost of tax payments, *tax administration* can impose additional costs on firms. Tax administration was a moderate or major constraint for more than 70 percent of firms in Central and Eastern Europe; for 65 percent of firms in CIS countries; for 63 percent of firms in LAC; 59

Table 2.2 Percentage of Firms That Rated Regulatory Constraints on Firms as "Major" or "Moderate"

Constraint	CEE	LAC	CIS	Africa	East Asia Developing	OECD	South Asia	MENA	East Asia NIC/China
High taxes	89.8	82.9	82.6	76.2	74.5	72.3	71.6	53.6	39.3
Tax administration and regulation	74.5	62.5	65.2	59.3	54.6	59.0	52.2	50.8	20.9
Customs/trade regulation	36.3	55.9	32.0	48.6	36.0	28.0	58.9	44.3	20.3
Labor regulation	18.2	52.5	33.7	38.0	35.2	47.7	60.0	32.6	27.4
Business registration	38.3	55.3	23.4	25.5	27.7	32.4	40.2	25.9	21.6
Environment	26.4	37.2	28.1	21.7	29.4	37.8	43.7	24.1	17.1
Foreign exchange/ currency	29.8	33.1	20.9	36.1	35.2	19.1	40.5	26.1	17.8
Fire/safety regulation	22.1	28.5	21.6	15.9	29.4	29.8	27.4	21.6	12.2

percent of firms in Africa and OECD nations; and for more than 50 percent of firms in South Asian, developing East Asian, and MENA countries. East Asian newly industrialized countries said they were remarkably unconstrained in general, with only 21 percent of firms rating tax administration as a serious constraint. As with high taxes, large firms were significantly, although not substantially, less constrained than SMEs.

Customs procedures and trade regulations imposed serious constraints on more than half of all firms in LAC and South Asia, 49 percent of firms in Africa, and 44 percent of firms in the MENA region. More than one-third of firms in the developing East Asia and the CEE regions rated this as a serious constraint. Small enterprises were significantly less constrained by customs and trade regulations than were large and medium-size firms.

The average waiting time for goods to be processed through ports and customs varied substantially, ranging from roughly 2 days in OECD nations, East Asia, and China (a firm's median wait was generally less than half a day), to more than 9 days in Central and Eastern Europe (a median of 5 days), 11 days in South Asia (a median of 7 days), and more than 16 days in Africa (a median of 10 days). These estimates exclude outliers, or processes that take more than 90 days.

The degree of constraint imposed by *labor regulations* varied sharply by region. About 60 percent of South Asian firms and 50 percent of Latin American firms said that labor relations were a major or moderate constraint. Nearly half the firms in OECD nations said they were a serious constraint, yet only 27 percent of firms in East Asia NIC/China and only 18 percent in Central and Eastern Europe agreed. Large firms were significantly more constrained than medium-size firms, and medium-size firms were significantly more constrained than small firms. Many countries have explicit size thresholds at which labor regulations must be applied, which helps to explain this pattern.

Business registration was a larger constraint on Latin American firms than it was on firms in other regions (see figure 2.14 and table 2.2). In Latin America, 55 percent of firms identified registration procedures as a serious constraint on their businesses. In South Asia and Central and Eastern Europe, this figure exceeded 35 percent. Because registration procedures are often perceived as an entry barrier to small firms, it is interesting that there was little difference in the responses of firms by size, with only a slightly higher percentage of large firms finding business registration to be a serious constraint.

Financing

The second most important constraint for all firms was financing. Firms in the CEE region were most likely to identify financing as a serious constraint, followed by those in CIS countries, then those in Africa, South

Figure 2.15 Financing Constraints, by Size of Firm

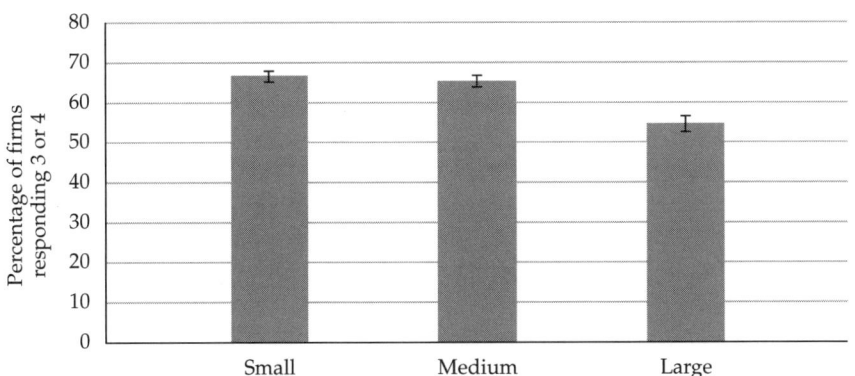

Notes: Error bars represent 95 percent confidence interval. Response options were: 1 = no obstacle; 2 = minor obstacle; 3 = moderate obstacle; 4 = major obstacle.

Asia, and Latin America. It is not surprising that whereas at least 50 percent of firms in all developing regions cited financing as a serious constraint, only 40 percent of firms in OECD countries found this to be so.

Financing was the second most important constraint to small and medium enterprises, but only the fourth in importance to large firms (see figure 2.15). Nevertheless, more than 50 percent of large firms identified financing as a major or moderate problem in their businesses.

As table 2.3 shows, *high interest rates* were a leading financial constraint across all regions; however, it is noteworthy that the majority of firms in industrial East Asia/China and OECD nations did not identify this as a serious constraint. This contrasts sharply with Latin America, where 88 percent of respondents identified interest rates as a leading constraint, as did 84 percent in South Asia and Africa, 81 percent in CIS countries, 80 percent in CEE nations, and 72 percent in developing East Asia. There was no significant difference in the responses of small, medium-size, and large firms on this issue.

Lack of access to long-term credit posed the next most important constraint, which was rated serious by more than half of all responding firms globally (this question was not posed in Africa and parts of the MENA region). This problem appears to seriously affect at least 60 percent of firms in CEE, South Asian, and Latin American nations, and more than 50 percent of firms in CIS and developing East Asian countries. Examined by size, half the large firms said that finding long-term credit was a serious problem, whereas 56 percent of medium-size firms and 58 percent of small firms found it to be a serious problem.

Table 2.3 Percentage of Firms That Rated Financing Constraints on Firms as "Major" or "Moderate"

Constraint	Africa	MENA	East Asia NIC/China	East Asia Developing	South Asia	LAC	OECD	CIS	CEE
High interest rates	83.5	67.4	40.3	72.5	83.9	87.6	47.8	80.6	79.5
Lack access to long-term loans	n.a.	n.a.	31.2	52.0	65.1	63.1	20.0	58.7	67.0
Collateral requirements	51.9	45.2	30.1	43.6	58.5	65.1	35.7	49.7	52.2
Bank paperwork	47.1	51.6	29.9	34.6	56.6	63.0	38.9	52.9	48.3
Inadequate credit information on clients	51.7	46.3	27.0	48.4	46.7	46.1	23.5	40.1	41.6
Special connections	38.2	33.3	26.3	39.6	44.5	46.5	26.5	35.1	43.1
Banks lack money to lend	28.4	33.0	20.6	52.2	35.1	39.1	14.3	37.4	46.8
Access to specialized export finance	44.9	39.8	15.1	33.7	36.4	34.7	16.5	35.5	38.8
Access to non-bank equity	43.1	36.2	13.0	32.6	34.9	35.6	18.1	38.3	42.0
Access to lease finance	38.2	29.3	13.1	34.9	32.9	34.1	19.3	32.7	48.9
Access to foreign banks	43.6	29.3	11.7	41.5	33.9	35.0	11.1	35.3	40.4
Corruption	23.5	27.4	19.0	45.1	28.9	18.6	5.7	24.3	29.0

n.a. Not asked.

Collateral requirements created a serious obstacle for 65 percent of Latin American respondents; 59 percent of South Asian respondents; and roughly half of those in Africa, CEE nations, and CIS countries. In sharp contrast, only 30 percent of respondents in China and NIC East Asia said that collateral requirements were a major or moderate constraint. As might be expected, this was a more serious issue for small enterprises than it was for large ones: 55 percent of small firms and 51 percent of medium-size firms rated this constraint as serious, whereas only 46 percent of large firms did so.

Bank paperwork was identified by more than 60 percent of enterprises in Latin America as a serious constraint, as it was for more than 50 percent of firms in South Asia, CIS, and the MENA region, with a slightly smaller percentage in CEE and Africa. Again, newly industrialized East Asia and China stand apart, with less than 30 percent of firms saying that paperwork was a serious constraint. Even in developing East Asia, this constraint was considered to be major or moderate by only 35 percent of firms. In general, the smaller the firm the more likely it was to find bank paperwork to be a business constraint.

Lack of credit information on customers was identified as a serious constraint by more than 40 percent of respondents in the global sample. This was considered a major or moderate constraint by more than 50 percent of firms in Africa. In all other regions except OECD and NIC East Asia/China, at least 40 percent of firms identified it as a serious constraint. Small firms were more likely to rate this as a serious constraint than were medium-size firms, and medium-size firms were more likely to do so than large firms.

As table 2.4 shows, *sources of finance* varied markedly by region and firm size. The WBES offered 11 possible sources of "fixed investment" financing and asked firms to estimate the percentage of financing from each. Unfortunately, in Africa and parts of the MENA region the question was posed to capture the leading sources of finance, rather than the amount of funding from each source.

Internal funds and retained earnings provided the leading source of financing in all regions. In South Asia and LAC, domestic commercial banks provided close to 20 percent of investment finance, and in developing East Asia and OECD nations, this figure was approximately 15 percent. According to respondents, only in Central and Eastern Europe did local banks fail to provide more than 10 percent of total investment finance. Family and friends were especially important sources of investment finance in developing East Asia and CIS countries, accounting for an average of 10 percent and 9 percent, respectively. Supplier credit was a relatively important issue in Latin America and East Asia/China. Equity or sale of stock provided an average of more than 5 percent of finance in

Table 2.4 Source of Firms' Fixed Invested Financing, by Region and Regional Group

Source	East Asia NIC/ China	East Asia Developing	South Asia	LAC	OECD	CIS	CEE
Internal funds/ retained earnings	48.3	33.9	26.5	43.2	39.1	53.9	70.5
Local commercial banks	11.6	15.7	18.5	19.8	14.6	11.4	4.8
Family/friends	3.3	9.9	6.3	4.3	2.3	8.6	7.3
Supplier credit	7.9	3.2	2.5	10.2	4.8	4.6	5.8
Equity, sale of stock	5.8	2.7	6.4	3.2	8.5	8.6	1.4
Foreign banks	3.3	4.8	2.6	4.0	1.5	2.1	0.6
Leasing arrangement	2.1	0.7	1.3	1.3	3.3	3.6	2.6
Investment funds/ special development finance	2.6	1.2	4.4	2.2	2.3	1.7	1.3
Other state sources	0.6	0.4	0.8	0.9	2.0	4.6	7.4
Moneylenders	2.9	1.7	1.1	1.1	2.3	2.5	1.6
Other	1.1	1.8	5.5	2.9	1.5	1.4	1.4

Note: Percentage of financing obtained from the source.

CIS countries (perhaps because of the inclusion of privatized firms in the sample), OECD countries, South Asia, East Asia, and China. "Other state sources" (meaning sources other than public investment funds or development finance funds) were important only in CEE and CIS countries.

SMEs in the sample relied less on commercial banks for investment finance than did large firms; they depended more on internal funds and retained earnings (see table 2.5). Small firms got less state support than did medium-size and large firms, but they received much more financing from family and friends.

In Africa, self-finance appeared to be the most common source of finance, followed by commercial banks and a firm owner's own capital or equity (see table 2.6). Family and friends were the most important source of financing for small firms. All sizes of firms benefited from supplier credit, but this was more common among SMEs than among large firms. Foreign banks often played a leading role in financing for large firms.

Table 2.5 Sources of Fixed Invested Financing, by Size of Firm

Source	Small (%)	Medium (%)	Large (%)
Internal funds/retained earnings	50.75	50.90	42.78
Local commercial banks	10.18	14.79	17.68
Moneylenders	2.36	1.44	0.99
Leasing arrangement	2.03	2.62	1.86
Equity, sale of stock	4.38	4.89	4.72
Foreign banks	0.72	2.76	6.92
Other state sources	0.71	5.63	4.33
Supplier credit	5.31	7.38	6.16
Investment funds/special development finance	1.20	2.24	2.70
Other	1.50	1.77	3.50
Family/friends	11.78	3.09	1.19

Table 2.6 First and Second Most Important Sources of Financing in Africa, by Size of Firm

Source	Small (%)	Medium (%)	Large (%)
Commercial banks	18.83	22.08	24.23
Development banks	5.40	7.33	8.26
Equity/own capital	13.42	14.01	13.40
Family/friends	9.56	1.50	2.67
Foreign banks	2.52	4.29	9.18
Leasing	3.26	3.84	1.71
Moneylenders	2.76	0.40	1.12
Self-finance	33.54	37.10	33.26
Supplier credit	8.34	7.78	4.81
Other	2.39	1.69	1.38

Policy Instability and Uncertainty

Policy instability and uncertainty, the third most important constraint cited by firms, varied substantially by region, but less by firm size. At one extreme, more than 70 percent of firms in South Asia, CEE nations, and developing East Asia found policy uncertainty/instability to be a serious constraint, with firms in LAC, MENA, and CIS also giving this issue a serious rating (see figure 2.16).

At the other extreme, only 26 percent of firms in NIC East Asia and China identified this as a major or moderate constraint, whereas 37 percent of firms in OECD countries did so. Medium-size firms were most

Figure 2.16 Policy Instability, by Region and Regional Group

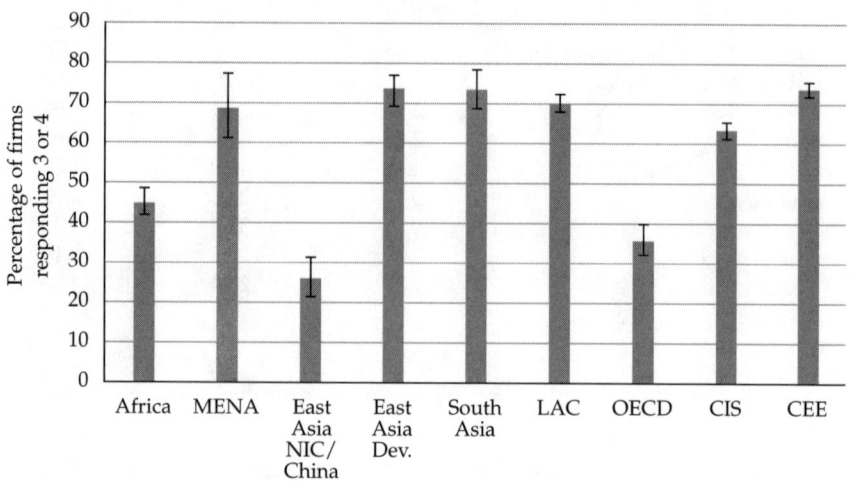

Notes: Error bars represent 95 percent confidence interval. Response options were: 1 = no obstacle; 2 = minor obstacle; 3 = moderate obstacle; 4 = major obstacle.

likely to find policy instability constraining, whereas large firms were significantly less likely to identify themselves as constrained than SMEs as a group, although by a small margin.

Macroeconomic policy instability can be seen as one element contributing to uncertainty. The constraints of inflation and exchange rate uncertainty are related, and concern about inflation somewhat echoed concern about policy instability by region. As figure 2.17 shows, firms in CEE countries were far more likely to find inflation a serious constraint; approximately 85 percent did so. Between 60 percent and 70 percent of firms in South Asia, developing East Asia, Latin America, and Africa found inflation to be constraining, with firms in CIS countries and MENA also providing high percentages. Large firms were significantly less likely to identify inflation as a major or moderate constraint than were small and medium-size firms.

As shown in figure 2.18, exchange rate uncertainty follows a slightly different pattern, but with important similarities. More than 70 percent of CEE firms found that exchange rate uncertainty was a serious constraint, more than 60 percent of firms from developing East Asia and Latin America found it so, and more than 50 percent of firms from MENA and South Asia identified it as a major or moderate constraint. By contrast, around 25 percent of firms in newly industrialized East Asia and OECD countries found the exchange rate to be a problem. Medium-size firms appeared most sensitive to exchange rate problems, with small firms a bit less so and large firms the least constrained.

Figure 2.17 Inflation, by Region and Regional Group

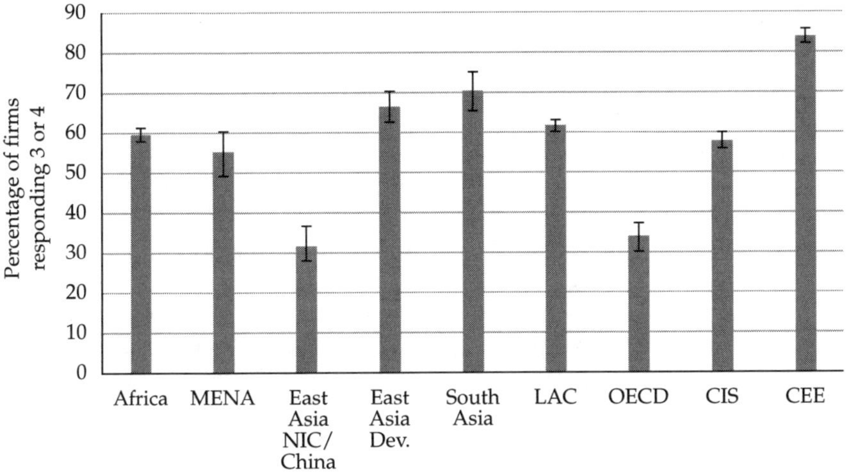

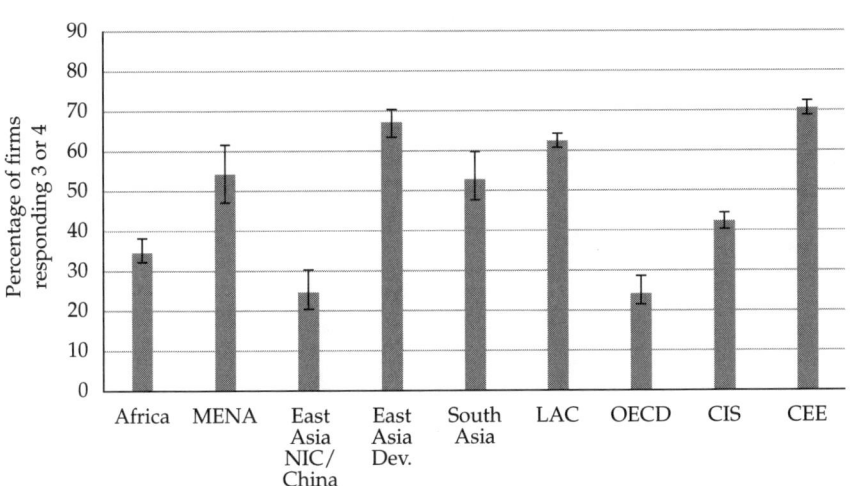

Notes: Error bars represent 95 percent confidence interval. Response options were: 1 = no obstacle; 2 = minor obstacle; 3 = moderate obstacle; 4 = major obstacle.

Figure 2.18 Exchange Rate, by Region and Regional Group

Notes: Error bars represent 95 percent confidence interval. Response options were: 1 = no obstacle; 2 = minor obstacle; 3 = moderate obstacle; 4 = major obstacle.

Another dimension of policy uncertainty/instability is associated with the predictability, transparency, and consistency with which governments are perceived to generate economic and financial policies, as well as supportive laws and regulations that affect firms. Figure 2.19 shows the percentage of firms in each region that found changes in economic and financial policies unpredictable to some degree (as opposed to firms finding them predictable to some degree). More than 70 percent of firms in CEE nations and more than 60 percent in CIS countries and developing East Asia found economic and financial policies unpredictable. Some 50 percent of firms in Latin America and more than 40 percent in South Asia saw these policies as unpredictable.

As table 2.7 shows, nearly three-quarters of the firms in CEE and Africa rated changes in rules, laws, and regulations affecting them as unpredictable. In CIS countries, two-thirds of firms rated these changes as unpredictable. In developing East Asia, Latin America, and MENA more than half of firms did so, as did 49 percent of firms in South Asia. Even in OECD nations, 45 percent of firms rated changes in the rules unpredictable. In East Asia less than 30 percent of firms did so.

Firms were also asked to evaluate the direction of change in the predictability of rules, policies, and regulations. The least encouraging result was in developing East Asia, where 41 percent of firms believed that predictability had declined; more than a third of surveyed firms in CEE and CIS agreed with this. Firms in OECD nations and East Asia NIC and

Figure 2.19 Predictability of Changes in Economic and Financial Policies "Which Materially Affect Your Business"

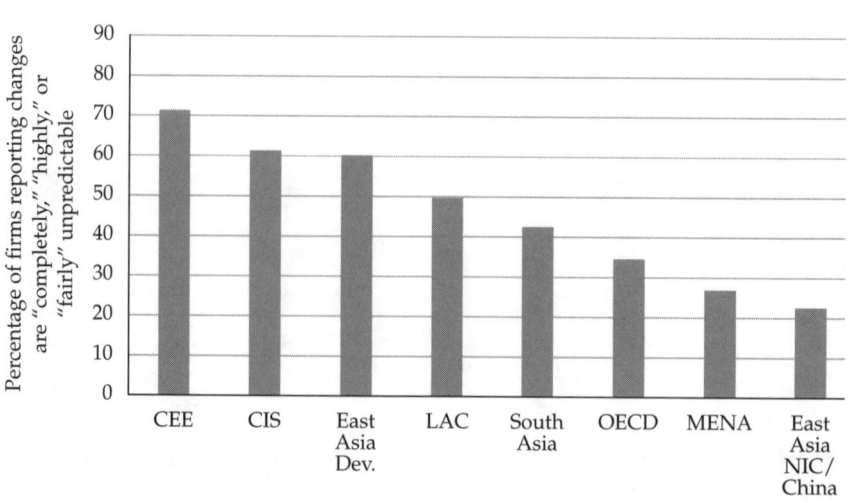

Table 2.7 Legal and Regulatory Predictability and Transparency, by Region and Regional Group

Region or regional group	Predictability of laws[a]	Evolution of predictability of laws and regulations over three years[b]	Firms notified in advance[c]
Africa	74	n.a.	37
CEE	74	37	68
CIS	66	35	60
East Asia Developing	59	41	28
MENA	52	25	26
LAC	52	26	57
South Asia	49	29	39
OECD	45	14	31
East Asia NIC/China	29	14	24

n.a. Not asked.
a. Percentage of firms responding "fairly," "highly," or "completely" unpredictable.
b. Percentage of firms responding "somewhat" or "much less" predictable.
c. Percentage of firms responding "seldom" or "never."

China saw the least decline in this area, with only 14 percent of firms noting deterioration in the predictability of rules and regulations.

Finally, the WBES measured one of the simplest steps governments could take to improve the predictability of policy change: notifying firms in advance of changes that affect them. In this regard, firms in CEE, CIS, and Latin American countries clearly fared worse than those in other regions, with 68 percent, 60 percent, and 57 percent of firms, respectively, reporting that they were seldom or never notified in advance of changes affecting them.

Large firms were less likely to find rules, laws, and regulations unpredictable and were less likely to perceive deterioration in the predictability of laws and regulations over the preceding three years (table 2.8). Whereas 57 percent of small firms said they were seldom or never notified in advance, 49 percent of medium-size firms gave such a negative assessment, and only 39 percent of large firms did so.

Two additional measures of transparency and consistency of policies and laws as experienced by firms are the availability of laws and regulations affecting firms and the consistency of the interpretation of laws and regulations. If laws and regulations are unavailable, this may contribute to a perception of policy uncertainty. Likewise, if the interpretation of

Table 2.8 Legal and Regulatory Predictability and Transparency, by Size of Firm

Size of firm	Predictability of laws[a] (%)	Evolution of predictability of laws and regulations over three years[b] (%)	Firms notified in advance[c] (%)
Small	64	34	57
Medium	61	29	49
Large	55	23	39

a. Percentage of firms responding "fairly," "highly," or "completely" unpredictable.
b. Percentage of firms responding "somewhat" or "much less" predictable.
c. Percentage of firms responding "seldom" or "never."

laws and regulations is inconsistent, rules affecting firms may appear unstable. The majority of firms agreed that laws and regulations affecting them were easily available. Companies in developing East Asia fared worse in this regard, with 39 percent of firms disagreeing. In Latin American, South Asian, and OECD countries, approximately one-third of firms disagreed. More than a quarter of firms in African, CEE and CIS nations disagreed; this figure is lower in the MENA region. Small firms found information on laws and regulations less available than did medium-size and large firms by a significant margin, with 36 percent of small firms disagreeing that they were easily available, versus 28 percent of medium firms and only 24 percent of large firms responding in the same manner.

Approximately half the firms in LAC and CIS countries disagreed that rules and laws are consistently interpreted, closely followed by 45 percent of OECD firms that disagreed, as do 42 percent of firms in South Asia, 40 percent of firms in developing East Asia, 37 percent of firms in CEE nations, and 36 percent of firms in Africa. Large firms found more consistency in the interpretation of laws and regulations than did medium-size and small firms.

The final constraint was whether government listens to the business perspective in the formulation of legal and policy reform. The survey question was: "In case of important changes in laws or policies affecting my business operation the government takes into account concerns voiced either by me or by my business association." In transitional European countries, MENA nations, and Latin America, the majority of firms suggested that this is a relatively rare event, but it was more common in Asia.

Corruption

This section first focuses on traditional measures of corruption, namely administrative/bureaucratic bribery and such related forms. Chapter four discusses the "grand corruption" of state capture, cases in which firms can affect laws, policies, and regulations to their advantage by providing officials with illicit payments.

Corruption was identified as a major or moderate business constraint by approximately half of the sample, with more than 70 percent of firms in South Asia and nearly as many in developing East Asia ranking this as an important obstacle (see figure 2.20). Two-thirds of the firms in MENA nations and 64 percent in Africa found corruption a serious constraint, as did 58 percent in LAC and more than half the firms in Central and Eastern Europe. In CIS countries, 47 percent of firms said that corruption was a major or moderate constraint. By contrast, only 20 percent of firms in the NIC East Asia and China and 17 percent of firms in OECD countries found corruption an important constraint. The reader should note that this general constraint question was the only question on corruption that could be posed in China. The consultant carrying out the survey reported that surveys are subject to rigorous censorship by the State statistics agency and that posing detailed questions on corruption would not only

Figure 2.20 Corruption, by Region and Regional Group

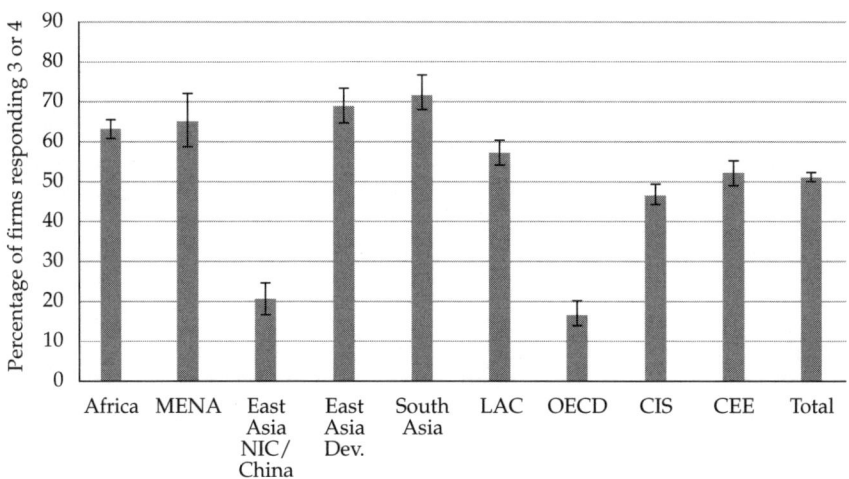

Notes: Error bars represent 95 percent confidence interval. Response options were: 1 = no obstacle; 2 = minor obstacle; 3 = moderate obstacle; 4 = major obstacle.
Total = average for all firms in the WBES sample.

invoke censorship, but might also derail the entire survey and even threaten the license of the consultant to carry out further survey work.

Small firms perceived corruption as a statistically significantly greater obstacle than medium-size or large firms, with 54 percent finding it a serious obstacle, compared with 50 percent of medium-size firms and 47 percent of large firms.

Although corruption can take many forms, the most readily observable to most firms is bribery by enterprises. Respondents were asked if it was common for firms "in their line of business to have to pay some irregular 'additional payments' to get things done." In South Asia and developing East Asia, more than 60 percent of firms said this was always, mostly, or frequently the case. In Africa, more than half of firms reported that such payments were at least frequently required. In MENA and Central and Eastern Europe countries, approximately one-third of the firms responded this way. In CIS nations and Latin America, more than a quarter of firms agreed. Only in OECD countries and East Asia (not including China, where corruption questions could not be asked) could this response be described as rare—only 12 percent of OECD firms and 11 percent of firms in newly industrialized East Asia picked these three most frequent response categories. By firm size, 40 percent of small enterprises chose the three most frequent response categories, as opposed to 34 percent of medium-size enterprises and 31 percent of small firms.

Frequency does not by itself represent the severity of corruption as a constraint to business. One aspect of severity is the uncertainty that discretion and rent seeking may introduce about the cost of additional payments. In some regions the "price" of getting things done is both well established and well known. For example, as table 2.9 shows, 70 percent of respondents in LAC responded that they always, mostly, or frequently knew in advance how much to pay officials informally, followed by 60 percent of firms in developing East Asia, 50 percent of those in South Asia, 48 percent of those in CEE countries, and 46 percent of those in CIS nations (this question was not asked in Africa and some MENA countries). Although large firms were less likely to find irregular payments necessary, they were somewhat more likely to know in advance how much to pay.

Equally important is whether or not the service "paid for" informally is delivered as promised. Some 83 percent of firms in South Asia reported that it always, mostly, or frequently was delivered as promised, 76 percent of firms in developing East Asia agreed, as did 75 percent of firms in CIS and 73 percent in CEE nations. This contrasts sharply with firms in Latin America and Africa, where only about one-third of firms said services were delivered as promised.

Table 2.9 Irregular Payments for Public Services, by Region and Regional Group

Region or regional group	Irregular additional payments made to government "to get things done"	Advance knowledge of amount of additional payment	Service delivered as agreed if additional payment made	If payment made to one official, another government official will request payment for same service	If government official acts against rules, can go to supervisor and get correct treatment without recourse to unofficial payment
South Asia	65	50	83	46	32
East Asia Developing	62	60	76	60	0.26
Africa	52	n.a.	33	n.a.	n.a.
MENA	36	42	53	26	28
CEE	33	48	73	28	36
CIS	29	46	75	35	38
LAC	28	70	32	70	69
OECD	12	26	62	17	45
East Asia NIC/China	11	22	42	10	25
Total	36	53	59	45	45

n.a. Not asked.
Note: Percentage of firms responding "always," "mostly," or "frequently" (as opposed to "sometimes," "seldom," or "never").

As shown in table 2.10, small firms found service delivery after bribery to be more reliable than did medium-size firms (62 percent and 58 percent, respectively), and medium-size firms were more likely to find this reliable than large firms (58 percent and 50 percent, respectively). Additional uncertainty related to corruption may arise if additional requests for payment are received after the initial informal payment has been made. Of the regions in which this question was asked, LAC and developing East Asia were the worst in this regard: 70 percent and 60 percent of firms, respectively, responded that once a payment had been made to one official, another official would always, mostly, or frequently request payment for the same service.

Except in Africa, parts of MENA, and China, the WBES survey asked whether a firm could appeal to a superior and receive correct treatment without recourse to an informal payment when an official acted against the rules. In Latin America, 69 percent of firms said this was always, mostly, or frequently the case, as did 45 percent of firms in OECD countries. In CIS countries, 38 percent of firms thought this was at least frequently possible, as did 36 percent of firms in CEE nations. However, East Asia (both regions) appeared not to invite such appeals, and only about a quarter of firms in either NIC countries or developing East Asia believed this was at least frequently possible. The perception of whether an appeal can be made successfully without a bribe rose dramatically with firm size: only 38 percent of small firms said they could appeal to a superior and obtain correct treatment without recourse to informal payments, but 48

Table 2.10 Irregular Additional Payments Made to Government, by Size of Firm

Question	Small	Medium	Large
Irregular additional payments made to government	40	34	31
Advance knowledge of amount of additional payment	53	52	59
Service delivered as agreed if additional payment made	62	58	50
If payment made to one official, another government official will request payment for same service	44	45	51
If government official acts against rules, can go to superior and get correct treatment without recourse to unofficial payment	38	48	53

Note: Percentage of firms responding "always," "mostly," or "frequently" (as opposed to "sometimes," "seldom," or "never").

Table 2.11 Percentage of Revenues Paid in Unofficial Payments to Public Officials, by Region and Regional Group

Region or regional group	Percentage of revenues paid in unofficial payments to public officials	Percentage of firms responding "0 percent"
Africa	n.a.	n.a.
MENA	n.a.	n.a.
CEE	5.5	0.9
South Asia	5.0	18.8
East Asia Developing	4.6	22.7
CIS	3.4	3.4
LAC	2.0	58.0
East Asia NIC	0.6	86.3
OECD	0.6	83.0
Average	3.0	38.7

n.a. Not asked.
Note: Scale of 1 to 7.
Average = average for the global sample weighted by firms, not regions.

percent of medium-size firms and 53 percent of large firms said this was at least frequently possible.

Aside from the frequency of payment, the severity of bribery as a problem may be influenced by the cost of bribes. Frequent payments could in theory be quite small; on the other hand, infrequent payments could be quite large. So WBES inquired (except in Africa, parts of MENA, and China) about the total percentage of revenues paid to public officials as "unofficial" payments. As table 2.11 shows, on average (using response category midpoints and a value of 33.3 percent for the category "over 25 percent"), payments were highest in CEE countries (5.5 percent of revenues), South Asia (5 percent), and developing East Asia (4.6 percent). Firms in CIS countries reported unofficial payments costing 3.4 percent of sales, while those in LAC said they cost 2 percent. It is worth noting that 86.3 percent of firms in NIC East Asia, 83 percent of firms in OECD countries, and 58 percent of firms in Latin America reported paying 0 percent of their revenues in bribes. In contrast, only 0.9 percent of firms in Central and Eastern Europe and 3.4 percent of firms in CIS countries reported zero payments. Payments averaged 3.8 percent of revenues for small firms, 2.7 percent for medium-size firms, and 1.7 percent for large firms, implying a regressive "tax" on revenues.

The amount of these payments is clearly associated with the degree to which firms find corruption constraining. For example, as shown in table 2.12, of firms that found corruption no obstacle or a minor obstacle are compared to those that found it a moderate or major obstacle, 78 percent

of the less-constrained group paid less than 1 percent of their sales in unofficial payments, but 51 percent of firms in the more constrained group
paid more than 1 percent of their sales in informal payments. Each category higher than 1 percent of sales for bribes contains a higher percentage of
the more-constrained group. Incidentally, a higher corruption score is not
only associated with higher average bribe payments, but also with a higher frequency of bribe payments and longer customs delays (see table 2.13).

Petty corruption through bribes is only one form of corruption. Two
further dimensions captured by WBES are payments for the award of
government contracts and influence over policy. Firms were asked
whether they had paid bribes for public procurement contracts or not,
and the percentage of the government contract value they had to offer as
an informal payment to secure a contract. Because many firms do not do
business with the public sector (and others did not respond to this sensitive question), the responses need to be assessed with particular caution.
However, the average findings are indicative for the overall sample in

Table 2.12 Percentage of Annual Revenues in Unofficial Payments

Rating	0	<1	1–1.99	2–9.99	10–12	13–25	>25
No obstacle – minor obstacle	53.7	24.5	8.8	8.0	2.9	1.1	1.0
Moderate – major obstacle	27.0	22.0	14.5	19.1	11.0	4.6	1.7
Overall average	40.0	23.2	11.7	13.7	7.1	2.9	1.3

Note: Scale of 1 to 7.

Table 2.13 Corruption, Payments, and Customs Delays

Corruption score[a]	Percentage of revenues per annum in unofficial payments[b]	Time delay with respect to imports	Firms commonly pay irregular payments[c]
1	1.5	10.6	5.2
2	2.3	11.4	4.3
3	2.8	13.5	3.7
4	2.9	13.8	3.4

a. Corruption score = 1 = no obstacle; 2 = minor; 3 = moderate; 4 = major obstacle.
b. Scale of 1 to 7: 1 = 0 percent; 2 = <1 percent; 3 = 1–1.99 percent; 4 = 2–9.99
percent; 5 = 10–12 percent; 6 = 13–25 percent; 7 = >25 percent.
c. Scale of 1 to 6: 1 = always; 2 = mostly; 3 = frequently; 4 = sometimes; 5 =
seldom; 6 = never.

that 45 percent of the respondent firms in the 80 countries surveyed admitted the need to provide such bribes and said that, on average, they paid as a bribe about 11 percent of the contract's value.

A further dimension of corruption is the potential for influencing the policies, regulations, and laws of the state. (In its extreme form, misgovernance is manifested through state capture. This was measured and analyzed for transition economies in the BEEPS component of the WBES, which is discussed in chapter four, box 4.2.) The WBES asked firms in all regions whether they had influence at the national level to affect laws and regulations that related to them (which in most instances could be thought of as legitimate and legal means, as opposed to state capture). The question was: "When a new law, rule, regulation, or decree is being discussed that could have a substantial impact on your business, how much influence does your firm typically have at the national level of government on the content of that law, rule, regulation or decree?"

As shown in table 2.14, separate responses were recorded for the executive branch, for the legislature, for the ministerial level, and for regulatory agencies. Firms in South Asia and developing East Asia were particularly confident of their ability to influence laws affecting them. In South Asia, more than half the responding firms responded that they could influence executives at the national and ministerial levels and more than 40

Table 2.14 Influence on Laws at the National Government Level, by Region and Branch

Region or regional group	"Does your firm have influence on the content of laws at the national level of government?"			
	Executive	Legislature	Ministry	Regulatory agency
Africa	n.a.	n.a.	n.a.	n.a.
MENA	n.a.	n.a.	n.a.	n.a.
East Asia NIC/China	34	30	33	29
East Asia Developing	44	43	44	50
South Asia	56	35	52	43
LAC	17	14	18	20
OECD	19	20	18	21
CIS	10	10	14	11
CEE	13	12	12	15
Total	17	16	18	19

n.a. Not asked.
Note: Percentage of firms responding "always," "mostly," or "frequently" (as opposed to "sometimes," "seldom," or "never").
Total = average for all firms in WBES sample.

percent thought they could influence regulatory agencies. In developing East Asia, half of the firms believed they could influence regulatory agencies and more than 40 percent suggested they could influence their government's executive branch, legislative branch, and individual ministries.

As table 2.15 shows, large firms were more likely to identify themselves as having influence at the national level than small or medium-size firms. It should be noted, however, that the number of firms reporting themselves as influential is only one relevant dimension of this issue: In many countries just a few enormously powerful firms can wield influence throughout the economy. The impact of firms' influence on governments may be less a function of the number of firms having influence and more a function of the relative influence each can wield. At the extreme, if all firms were equally influential, the overall impact of their influence could be expected to be more neutral.

Corruption is, of course, a two-way street—firms may benefit in certain ways from their ability to corrupt officials who might otherwise enforce laws or implement programs in a manner less favorable to them. In theory, this tendency may mute the adverse evaluation of corruption in some regions as a constraint to business—that is, if firms get what they want from corruption, they may not identify corruption as a constraint.

One manifestation of weak governance, by virtue of corruption or lax enforcement, is the degree to which firms comply with laws, including tax laws. WBES asked firms to estimate the percentage of sales that typical enterprises reported to tax authorities (see table 2.16). Less than 10 percent of the firms in MENA estimated that firms reported 100 percent of their sales. Only in OECD did a majority of responding firms report average underreporting to be less than 10 percent of sales. In MENA, 74 percent of firms estimated underreporting of sales to exceed 20 percent of total revenues. In developing East Asia, this response came from 63 percent

Table 2.15 Influence on Laws at the National Government Level, by Size of Firm

	"Does your firm have influence on the content of laws at the national level of government?"			
Size of firm	Executive	Legislature	Ministry	Regulatory agency
Small	0.12	0.12	0.13	0.14
Medium	0.17	0.15	0.17	0.20
Large	0.28	0.26	0.29	0.30

Note: Percentage of firms responding "always," "mostly," or "frequently" (as opposed to "sometimes," "seldom," or "never").

Table 2.16 Estimated Percentage of Sales Reported to Tax Authority, by Region and Regional Group

Region or regional group	Percentage of sales						
	100	90–99	80–89	70–79	60–69	50–59	<50
Africa	29.28	14.06	8.66	8.35	6.26	5.77	3.50
MENA	5.12	14.57	6.69	10.24	14.96	18.11	16.93
East Asia Developing	21.10	7.28	8.33	9.28	5.49	9.81	19.94
East Asia NIC/China	33.89	6.31	5.32	1.66	0.66	4.32	21.93
CEE	34.51	12.96	12.73	7.11	4.83	9.89	7.16
CIS	31.05	10.99	8.52	6.56	3.87	5.89	5.94
LAC	38.08	5.71	9.21	7.34	5.52	5.66	14.20
South Asia	31.40	14.88	6.06	2.75	4.41	9.64	7.71
OECD	49.06	15.95	8.03	4.73	2.42	1.76	2.75
Total	32.96	10.93	9.13	7.01	4.99	6.92	9.33

Total = average for all firms in the WBES sample.

Table 2.17 Percentage of Sales Reported to Tax Authority, by Size of Firm

Size of firm	Percentage of sales						
	100	90–99	80–89	70–79	60–69	50–59	<50
Small	25.83	10.30	9.78	8.05	5.38	8.17	11.48
Medium	36.05	11.68	9.30	6.72	5.06	6.52	7.94
Large	41.43	10.70	7.53	5.45	4.10	5.19	7.79
Total	32.96	10.93	9.13	7.01	4.99	6.92	9.33

Total = average for all firms in the WBES sample.

of firms. In newly industrialized East Asia this response came from 55 percent of the firms.

As table 2.17 shows, underreporting was clearly perceived to be greater among small firms than either medium-size or large firms. Only 25.8 percent of small firms said that firms like them report 100 percent of sales, and 63 percent said that average underreporting exceeded 20 percent of total sales.

3

Quality of
Public Services

The quality of public services is a key dimension of the business environment and an indicator of the quality of governance, so WBES explored the general characteristics of government services and the qualities of individual services. One dimension of service is whether firms find government helpful to the conduct of business. In this regard, government was regarded as least helpful in transitional Europe: in Central and Eastern Europe, where 63 percent of firms found national government unhelpful and 53 percent found local government unhelpful; and in CIS countries, where 47 percent of firms found national government unhelpful and 43 percent found local government unhelpful (see table 3.1). Local government was considered slightly more unhelpful in Latin America and the Caribbean, where 44 percent of enterprises found it unhelpful. By sharp contrast, only 13 percent of MENA firms and 14 percent of developing East Asia firms found national government unhelpful. Helpfulness can be

Table 3.1 Government Helpfulness, by Region and Regional Group

Region or regional group	Helpfulness of national government	Helpfulness of local government
Africa	33	40
CEE	63	53
CIS	47	43
East Asia Developing	14	15
East Asia NIC/China	11	17
LAC	41	44
MENA	13	18
OECD	38	35
South Asia	32	34
Total	40	40

Note: Percentage of firms responding "mildly" or "very" unhelpful.
Total = average for all firms in the WBES sample.

interpreted negatively if it takes the form of favoritism or protection, so some would argue that a neutral response is the best outcome.

Government Efficiency

WBES explored both the overall efficiency of government in delivering services and the quality of individual services. More than 60 percent of firms in Central Europe, Latin America, and CIS countries believed government was to some extent inefficient in delivering services (table 3.2). Nearly 60 percent of South Asian firms also identified government as inefficient, and half of respondents in OECD countries regarded their governments as inefficient. Small firms had the most negative view of government efficiency in service delivery, followed by medium-size firms, with large firms providing the most favorable evaluation (see table 3.3).

Quality of Specific Public Services

As shown in figure 3.1, a majority of firms gave a negative evaluation of public health, parliament, and public works and roads. Between 40 percent and 50 percent of firms gave a negative evaluation of courts, police, education services, and central government leadership. More than a third

Table 3.2 Efficiency of Government Service Provision, by Region and Regional Group

Region or regional group	Percentage of firms that rated government service provision inefficient
CEE	70
LAC	63
CIS	63
South Asia	58
OECD	50
East Asia Developing	40
East Asia NIC/China	16

Table 3.3 Efficiency of Government Service Provision, by Size of Firm

Size of firm	Percentage of firms that rated government service provision inefficient
Small	0.62
Medium	0.58
Large	0.54

Figure 3.1 Quality and Integrity of Public Services, Global Average (Unweighted)

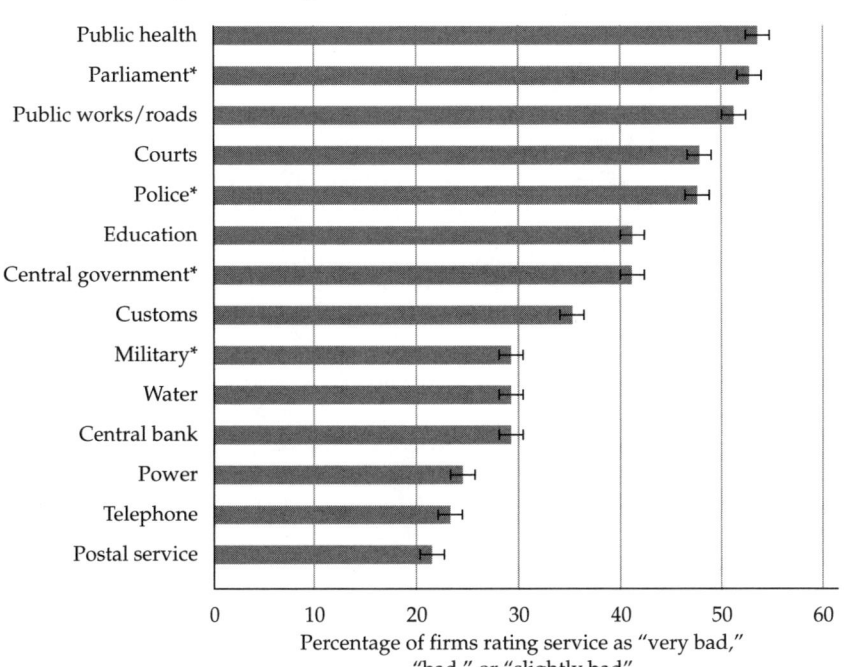

Percentage of firms rating service as "very bad," "bad," or "slightly bad"

Note: *Not asked in China because of government censorship policies.

gave negative ratings to customs. The most highly rated agencies were the postal service, telephone service, and electric power service, which were rated favorably by at least three-quarters of respondents.

By region, although some services were not evaluated in all regions, the average of services rated was lowest for Central European countries, followed by those in Africa, then South Asia and Latin America, and CIS countries. The most positive ratings average was assigned by firms in newly industrialized East Asia countries, followed by MENA countries (see table 3.4).

The regional results show sharp differences in perceptions of services. Hospital and health care services provide one clear example (see figure 3.2). In four regions, CEE, LAC, Africa, and South Asia, more than half the respondents offered a negative evaluation of these services, with firms in CIS countries offering a similar response. These services were viewed favorably in NIC East Asia and China, and in developing East Asia and OECD countries at least two-thirds of firms rated these services favorably.

Table 3.4 Evaluation of Public Services, by Region and Regional Group

Public service	Africa	MENA	East Asia NIC/China	East Asia Developing	South Asia	LAC	OECD	CIS	CEE	Overall average
Postal service	32	7	7	9	26	26	25	13	26	22
Telephone	35	5	7	15	29	21	22	16	34	24
Power	39	9	8	19	48	26	12	17	32	25
Central bank	n.a.	n.a.	9	35	25	24	20	21	51	29
Water	43	14	9	25	39	28	14	25	37	29
Military*	32	10	7	26	9	32	22	21	50	29
Customs	38	14	8	32	47	37	21	30	49	35
Central government	34	3	n.a.	30	40	36	43	44	63	42
Education	50	16	11	25	50	54	37	30	50	42
Police*	57	14	12	37	61	58	26	38	63	48
Courts	39	21	15	34	35	59	42	55	57	48
Public works/roads	53	20	14	41	55	49	43	57	62	51
Parliament*	40	14	12	33	60	64	45	58	70	53
Public health	63	28	15	25	62	68	33	39	69	54

n.a. Not available.

Note: Percentage of firms that rate the service "slightly bad," "bad," or "very bad."

*Not asked in China because of government censorship policies.

Total = average for all firms in the WBES sample.

Ratings of parliaments also varied, although with a different pattern (see figure 3.3). Some 70 percent of firms in Central and Eastern Europe, more than 60 percent of firms in LAC and South Asia, and nearly 60 percent of those in CIS countries gave a negative evaluation to their parlia-

Figure 3.2 Public Health Care Service/Hospitals, by Region and Regional Group

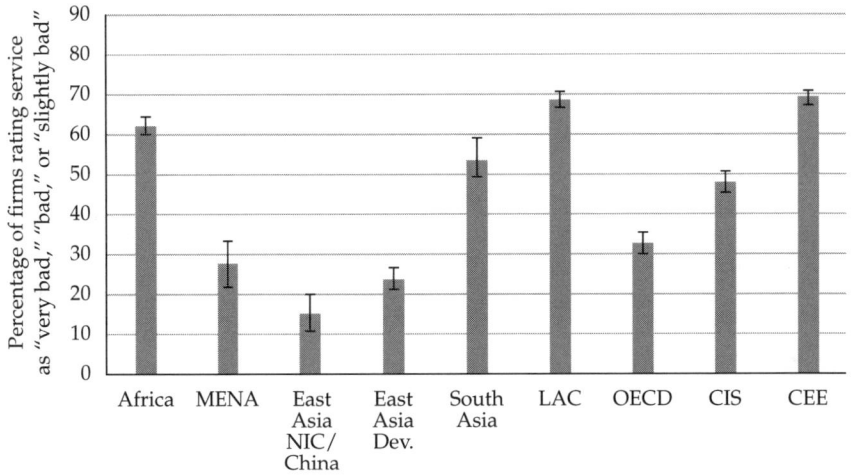

Note: Error bars represent 95 percent confidence interval.

Figure 3.3 Parliament, by Region and Regional Group

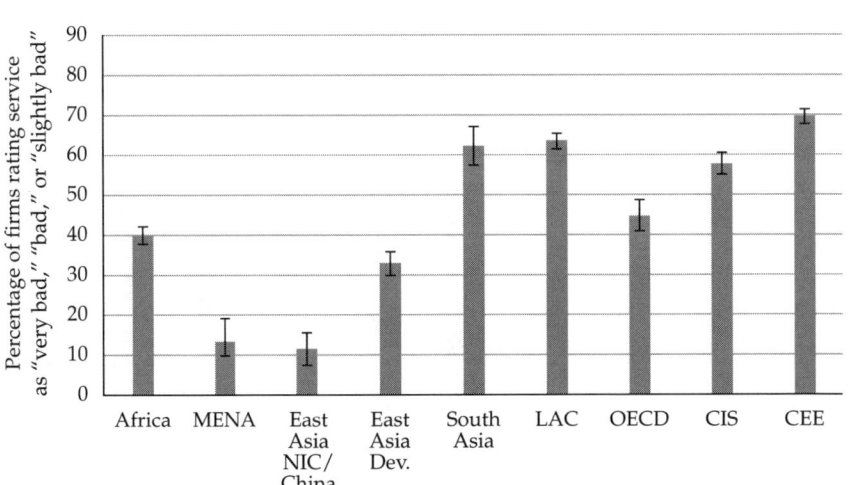

Note: Error bars represent 95 percent confidence interval.

ments. In contrast, evaluations of parliaments in newly industrialized East Asia and MENA were overwhelmingly favorable, with at least 85 percent of firms providing a rating of slightly good or better.

The next least favorably rated service was public works and roads (see figure 3.4). More than half of respondents in Central and Eastern Europe, South Asia, CIS countries, and Africa rated the quality of these services as poor. Just under half of Latin American firms held a similarly negative view. Only in newly industrialized East Asia/China and MENA countries were the ratings of this service category sharply positive, with more than 80 percent of responding firms providing a rating of slightly good or better.

The next most frequently negatively rated government service was the judiciary and courts, with more than half the firms in Latin American, CIS, and CEE countries rating the courts negatively (see figure 3.5). Surprisingly, more than 40 percent of firms in OECD countries gave courts a negative review, as did approximately 40 percent of respondents in Africa and South Asia.

WBES respondents also rated detailed characteristics of the courts, which sheds some light on the basis for these general ratings. The most obvious negative characteristic of courts was the speed at which they operate. Eighty-five percent of firms responded that courts were never, seldom, or only sometimes quick (as opposed to always, usually, or frequently). As table 3.5 shows, the most negative review of quickness was

Figure 3.4 Roads/Public Works, by Region and Regional Group

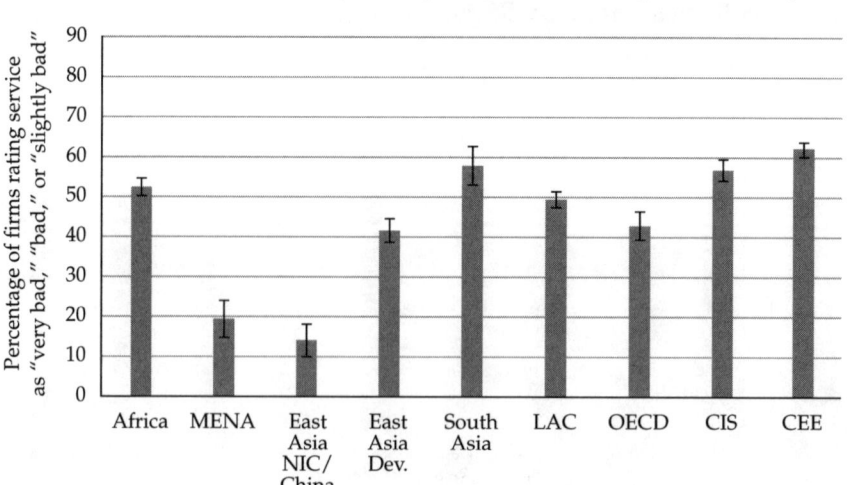

Note: Error bars represent 95 percent confidence interval.

Figure 3.5 Judiciary/Courts, by Region and Regional Group

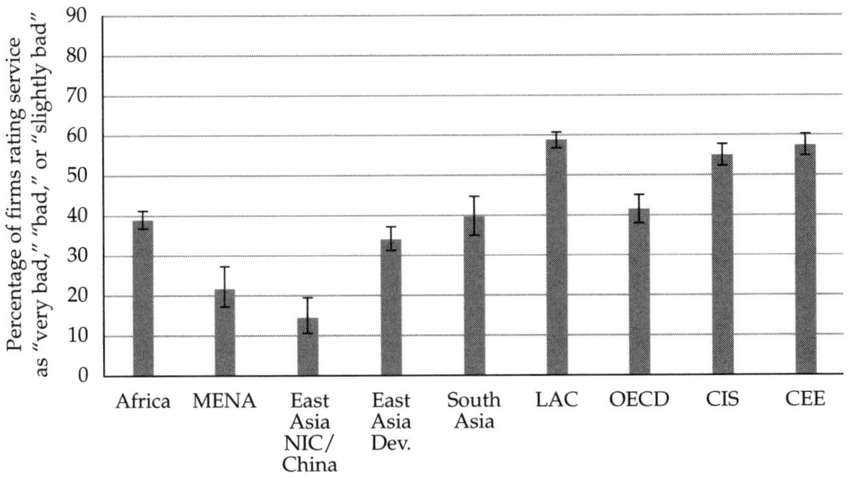

Note: Error bars represent 95 percent confidence interval.

in Latin America, where 94 percent of firms responded in the three least frequent categories, followed by Africa, where 86 percent of firms found courts infrequently quick. A second dimension in which courts were found wanting was consistency: 65 percent of firms across all regions found them never, seldom, or only sometimes consistent. Latin American firms held the dimmest view of their courts in this regard as well, with 79 percent reporting that courts were infrequently consistent. In Central and Eastern Europe, 78 percent of firms and 65 percent of those in CIS countries held a similarly negative view. Courts were regarded as never, seldom, or only sometimes affordable by 64 percent of firms in the sample, including 77 percent of OECD firms, 71 percent of LAC firms, and 65 percent of firms in CIS nations. Fifty-eight percent of firms rated courts in the three least frequent categories for honesty, led by 79 percent of CEE firms, and 70 percent of Latin American firms, as well as 59 percent of firms in developing East Asia and 57 percent of those in CIS nations. Fifty-seven percent of firms rated courts for being fair and impartial, led by firms in CEE countries (74 percent) and Latin America (70 percent). Finally, another 57 percent of firms rated courts' enforcement of judgments as happening never, seldom, or sometimes, including 68 percent of firms in CEE countries, 67 percent of firms in Latin America, and 59 percent of firms in developing East Asia.

Considered by company size, the overall percentage of firms giving a slightly bad, bad, or very bad rating to public services declined slightly with size, from 39 percent of small firms to 35 percent of large ones. Large firms evaluated parliament, central government, and the central bank considerably better than did small and medium-size firms with at least a 9 percentage-point difference in their negative ratings. They also had a

Table 3.5 Qualities of the Court System, by Region and Regional Group

Region or regional group	Fair and impartial	Honest	Quick	Affordable	Consistent	Decrees enforceable
Africa	47	52	86	58	59	50
MENA	23	23	47	23	26	29
East Asia NIC/ China	23	27	42	37	29	25
East Asia Developing	55	59	81	74	51	59
South Asia	31	37	81	61	48	47
LAC	70	70	94	71	79	67
OECD	48	38	87	77	59	49
CIS	56	57	90	65	65	56
CEE	74	79	80	57	78	68

Note: Percentage of firms responding "never," "seldom," or "sometimes" (as opposed to "always," "usually," or "frequently").

Table 3.6 Firms' Ratings of Public Services, by Size of Firm

	Small	Medium	Large	Average
Postal service	21	22	24	22
Telephone	23	24	22	24
Power	26	25	25	25
Central bank	33	30	20	29
Water	31	29	27	29
Military	31	30	26	29
Customs	37	35	32	35
Central government	46	42	33	42
Education	41	43	43	42
Police	49	48	46	48
Courts	50	48	44	48
Public works/roads	53	51	46	51
Parliament	55	55	46	53
Public health	54	55	55	54

Note: Percentage of firms rating the service as "slightly bad," "bad," or "very bad."
Average = average for all firms in the WBES sample.

more favorable view of roads and courts. It is not possible to judge from the data whether this was simply a difference in perception or whether large firms are better served by political institutions and certain public services. A number of services, including health, education, police, telephone, and postal services, received closely parallel ratings by firms of similar size.

4

Business and Governance Constraints and Enterprise Performance

This chapter explores the use of indicators derived from WBES in explaining firm-level outcomes. The first section uses econometric analysis to identify the correlates of reported firm-level growth and investment. The second section presents an important application of the data in analyzing "unofficialdom" (that is, a firm's hiding of output) and an example of the abundance of applications that such globally comparative data affords. The last section explores firm characteristics as they apply to the data.

The Relationship between Business and Governance Constraints and Enterprise Growth

In this section we turn to an empirical analysis of how constraints correlate to the microeconomic outcomes of sales growth and investment. We are interested in exploring whether constraints in the business environment, as perceived by enterprises, are associated with lower sales or investment growth. This analysis has important ramifications for policymakers because where enterprise growth correlates with the constraints to business, policies that remove these constraints could lead to productivity gains and economic growth.

To explore whether and how constraints in the business environment, as perceived by enterprises, are associated with sales and investment growth, we estimated two regression models that include the constraint rankings for key environment variables. We controlled for such firm attributes as size, export and foreign ownership status, and country differences. We recognize that the causality might run in the opposite direction; there might be simultaneity between constraints and growth, and some of the constraints may even be caused by factors inside the system itself. As a result, the regression estimates might be subject to bias. However, given the unique data provided by the WBES, our objective was to establish a clear empirical association between key business environment constraints and growth.

Two specifications were tested. In the first equation, the dependent variable was the sales growth over a three-year period (for example, from 1997 through 1999) reported by firms in the survey. This variable is regressed on such *key business environment attributes* as corruption, policy instability, taxes and regulations, and financial constraints; and on *firm-level attributes,* including firm size, age, export status, and foreign ownership. Firm attributes are all represented by indicator variables. In the survey, the main attributes of the business environment, such as financing, corruption, making policy changes, and taxes, were qualitative perceptions. To better quantify some of these variables, they were all converted to binary indicator variables (0,1). Thus, the coefficients on constraint scores can be interpreted as the associated difference in growth levels with variations in these conditions and, by inference, policy differences at the national level.

Corruption is measured as the frequency of additional payments made by enterprises on a scale of 0–1, with 0 representing the three least frequent responses on a six-point scale (never, rarely, sometimes) and 1 representing the three most frequent responses (always, usually, frequently). Similarly, consultation of businesses on legal and policy reform ("In case of important changes in laws or policies affecting my business operation the government takes into account concerns voiced either by me or by my business association") was represented by a binary variable representing frequency. A negative coefficient would reflect a negative relationship between a higher frequency of these variables and growth. High taxes and financing constraints were measured on a scale of 0–1, with 0 indicating a response of no obstacle or a minor obstacle, and 1 indicating a response of a moderate obstacle or a major obstacle. A negative sign on the coefficient of any of these constraint variables, as measured, would reflect the negative relationship between these constraints and growth.

Because the variables representing the perceptions of the environment are significantly correlated with each other, stepwise regression methods were employed to determine the most important constraints correlated with growth. Firm size, age, export, and foreign ownership status are represented by indicator variables. Finally, indicator variables were included to represent country effects—the reference country in table 4.1 is Albania. Because there were 80 countries and one territory in the sample, this required 80 country indicators (one for each country or territory other than Albania, which, owing to alphabetical ordering, served as the base case). Country control variables were used to pick up potentially omitted factors specific to a country that would influence the overall response (such as recent civil war or different culture).

Table 4.1 reports the estimated regression parameters. The results reveal two interesting findings. First, firm attributes, including firm size and the export status of firms, are positively and significantly associated with higher sales growth, but the age of the firm is negatively associated with growth. This finding is consistent with the literature (Batra and Tan, forthcoming; Roberts and Tybout 1996).

Second, and more important, the results indicate that several business constraints are significantly associated with sales growth (after controlling for country differences and variations in firm attributes), including age, size, export, and foreign ownership status. Financing, high taxes, and corruption (which are, on average, moderate to major constraints to businesses) are significantly and negatively associated with sales growth. Lack of or infrequent consultation of businesses on policies that affect

Table 4.1 Constraints on Firms' Growth—Dependent Variable: Sales Growth in Previous Three Years

Determinant	Estimate (t statistic)
Business constraints	
Financing	−4.63*
	(2.82)
High taxes	−2.04*
	(2.45)
Consultation of businesses	−1.61*
	(2.55)
Corruption	−3.95**
	(2.45)
Firm characteristics	
Medium-size firm	2.10
	(1.69)
Large firm	4.57**
	(2.33)
Newer firm (started since 1994)	−8.34*
	(7.58)
Exporter	19.64*
	(9.72)
Foreign investment	1.04
	(0.488)
Constant	14.82
	(1.31)
Adjusted R^2	0.12
Number of observations	4,560

**Significant at 5 percent; *significant at 10 percent level.
Note: Country indicators were included in the above regression. Estimates are available from the authors on request.

them also bear a negative relationship to growth. For example, the coefficient for finance suggests that a firm that identified itself as constrained to a moderate or major degree by financing, on average, reported a growth rate that is 4.63 percentage points lower than one that was not so constrained. A firm seriously constrained by corruption reported, on average, a growth rate 3.95 percent lower than one that was not so constrained.

In the second specification, the dependent variable was change in investment over a three-year period (for example, 1997 to 1999) reported by firms in the survey. As in the earlier model, this variable is regressed on such key business environment attributes as corruption, policy instability, taxes and regulations, and financing constraints, as well as such firm-level attributes as size, age, export status, and foreign ownership. As before, constraints were represented by indicator variables (0,1), where 0 represents no obstacle or a minor obstacle and 1 represents a moderate or major obstacle. The results of the regression are reported in table 4.2. Policy uncertainty in this regression is measured by changes in the predictability of government policies, laws, and regulations over the three years, where a 1 indicates no change or a decline in predictability and a zero indicates an improvement in predictability.

First, by analyzing the firm attributes, it is clear that younger firms and firms that export have, on average, higher investment growth than older firms and nonexporters. Among the business environment attributes, the results indicate that a decline in the predictability of changes in economic policies over the last three years, corruption, high taxes, and financing are significantly and negatively associated with investment growth.

Considered together, the implications of these findings are significant. At the most basic level they suggest that, controlling for a broad variety of factors, several of the constraints firms rated as most important are significantly related to the actual performance of firms. Second, they imply that, with other things being equal, countries with poor conditions in four categories (financing, corruption, high taxes, and consultation of business on rules and regulations) saw their existing businesses grow an average of 10.5 percentage points less than those with positive ratings in all of these categories. Countries with poor conditions in the areas of financing, high taxes, corruption, and policy predictability also saw their businesses grow an average of 10.5 percentage points less than those with positive ratings in all of these categories. This is at least strongly suggestive of the types of results obtainable with substantial improvements in policy. The difficult tasks of reforming taxes, financing, corruption, and policy predictability may take years, but the evidence suggests that higher growth and investment are associated with such improvements.

Table 4.2 Constraints on Firms' Growth—Dependent Variable: Investment Growth in Previous Three Years

Determinant	Estimate (t statistic)
Business constraints	
Financing	–2.46*
	(3.96)
High taxes	–1.69**
	(2.31)
Predictability of policies	–3.75*
	(2.55)
Corruption	–2.57***
	(1.77)
Firm characteristics	
Medium-size firm	2.30
	(1.52)
Large firm	2.07
	(1.02)
Newer firm (started since 1994)	–4.93*
	(4.83)
Exporter	10.62*
	(6.06)
Foreign investment	0.38
	(0.20)
Constant	46.34*
	(5.04)
Adjusted R^2	0.13
Number of observations	3,006

***Significant at 1 percent; **significant at 5 percent; *significant at 10 percent level.

Note: Country indicators were included in the above regression. Estimates are available from authors on request.

Behavioral Response of the Firm to Official Constraints: Determinants of Unofficialdom— An Econometric Application

The WBES results make clear that there is a spectrum of formality on the part of the responding firms, from the wholly official to the mostly unofficial (although all WBES firms are officially registered). A large share of officially registered firms hide at least a part of their output and thereby turn at least in part unofficial. The worldwide dataset on our survey firms permits us to test the extent to which companies are hiding output, and the importance of the various potential business environment conditions associated with their decisions to do so. We asked each firm to provide an estimate of the percentage of sales revenues that firms like their own report. Based on their responses, we inferred that the firms in the sample do not report 19 percent of their gross revenues. To illustrate the type of analysis made possible by the rich dataset generated by WBES, this section presents an analysis of the determinants of unofficial enterprise behavior.

It could be assumed that the decision of a firm to hide its output may be related to the low benefits it derives from operating officially and the low cost of crossing over to the unofficial economy. More specifically, we can draw from the framework used in Johnson, Kaufmann, and Shleifer (JKS) in 1997 for the unofficial economy in transition, which was subsequently extended for 69 countries worldwide (Johnson, Kaufmann, and Zoido-Lobatón 1999, and Friedman and others 2000). In the JKS model, a firm makes a rational economic choice whether to operate officially or unofficially based on the incentives it faces, which are determined by the government provision of, or failure to provide, public goods (such as rule of law and honesty). Against such a framework, we can test the WBES microeconomic dataset to determine the main determinants of the unofficial economy.

To do so, we performed ordinary least squares (OLS) regressions with this firm-level sample, including country effects. The basic econometric specifications shown in table 4.3 present the various possible determinants of the behavior of registered firms with regard to the unofficial economy. The analysis also employed "*kvetch* controls," not reported in the table (see box 4.1). A number of policy-related variables are shown to be significantly related to the extent of the firm's underreporting of revenues. On the economic and financial policy side, macroeconomic, regulatory, and tax constraints are significant; when these policies are below par a firm will tend to operate unofficially. Governance-related constraints are also important. In particular, corruption and some legal variables related to property rights protection—such as copyright violations—are significant in determining the propensity of a firm to operate unofficially.

The econometric investigation at the firm level also allows an examination of whether enterprise characteristics, controlling for policy and governance variables, also matter. As seen in table 4.3, small or medium-size firms that produce for the domestic market (nonexporters), lack foreign investment, and are located in large cities (but not necessarily in the capital) tend to engage more in unofficial activity. By contrast, the coefficients for de novo firms, sector dummies, and private ownership are insignifi-

Table 4.3 Underreported Revenues, Corruption, and Protection of Property Rights—Dependent Variable (Using Full Sample): Underreported Revenues (in Percentage, Sample Mean = 19 Percent)

Determinant	Estimate (t statistic)					
	1	2	3	4	5	6
Business constraints						
Financing	0.27	0.11	0.46	0.44	0.27	0.09
	(0.85)	(0.33)	(1.44+)	(1.32)	(0.79)	(0.25)
Inflation	–0.01	–0.03	0.07	0.01	–0.05	–0.09
	(–0.03)	(–0.12)	(0.31)	(0.04)	(–0.23)	(–0.37)
Policy instability	0.60	0.77	0.77	0.81	0.65	0.81
	(2.64***)	(3.24***)	(3.48***)	(3.55***)	(2.78***)	(3.30***)
Infrastructure	0.58	0.37	0.75	0.88	0.73	0.51
	(1.65+)	(0.98)	(2.15**)	(2.44**)	(2.00**)	(1.29)
Tax/regulatory	1.37	—	—	—	1.26	—
	(3.38***)	—	—	—	(2.97***)	—
Rule of law						
Bribery (percentage of	0.29	0.33	0.31	0.34	0.33	0.37
revenues)	(5.47***)	(5.53***)	(5.70***)	(6.17***)	(5.91***)	(5.97***)
Copyright violations	—	2.31	—	—	—	2.36
	—	(7.31***)	—	—	—	(7.11***)
Firm characteristics						
Private ownership	0.24	–0.52	0.23	0.25	0.24	–0.55
	(0.20)	(–0.39)	(0.19)	(0.21)	(0.20)	(–0.41)
Small firm[a]	4.35	4.28	4.40	4.50	4.47	4.54
	(4.43***)	(4.07***)	(4.48***)	(4.38***)	(4.35***)	(4.13***)
Medium-size firm[a]	0.93	1.18	0.97	0.84	0.78	1.07
	(1.05)	(1.25)	(1.09)	(0.91)	(0.85)	(1.09)
Newer firm (started	–0.14	–0.02	–0.13	–0.05	–0.07	0.10
since 1994)	(–0.28)	(–0.05)	(–0.26)	(–0.10)	(–0.13)	(0.18)
Exporter	–0.46	–1.02	–0.54	–1.00	–0.90	–1.16
	(–0.65)	(–1.33)	(–0.76)	(–1.32)	(–1.19)	(–1.41)
Foreign investment	–3.53	–3.24	–3.58	–3.40	–3.38	–3.06
	(–4.28***)	(–3.67***)	(–4.33***)	(–4.00***)	(–3.97***)	(–3.35***)
Location, small city[b]	–0.18	–0.13	–0.17	–0.09	–0.11	–0.07
	(–0.18)	(–0.12)	(–0.18)	(–0.08)	(–0.11)	(–0.07)
Location, large city[b]	1.62	1.41	1.61	1.87	1.87	1.72
	(1.87*)	(1.51+)	(1.87*)	(2.11**)	(2.11**)	(1.79*)
Manufacturing[c]	—	—	—	1.72	1.56	2.06
				(0.84)	(0.77)	(0.91)
Service[c]	—	—	—	–0.10	–0.04	1.65
				(–0.04)	(–0.02)	(0.62)

(continued on next page)

Table 4.3, *continued*

Determinant	Estimate (t statistic)					
	1	2	3	4	5	6
Agriculture[c]	—	—	—	–0.52	–0.57	0.55
				(–0.26)	*(–0.28)*	*(0.24)*
Construction[c]	—	—	—	1.98	1.87	2.16
				(0.91)	*(0.86)*	*(0.90)*
Adjusted R^2	.22	.23	.21	.22	.22	.23
Number of observations	4,775	4,166	4,781	4,386	4,381	3,802

***Significant at 1 percent; **significant at 5 percent; *significant at 10 percent;
[+]significant at 15 percent.
— Variable not used in this equation.
a. Large firms constitute the benchmark.
b. Location in capital constitutes the benchmark.
c. Other sectors constitute the benchmark.
Note: From the survey, business constraints were rated on a scale from 1 to 4, where
1 implies "no constraint" and 4 "major obstacle," These include inflation, financing, infrastructure, tax/regulation, and policy instability constraints, as well as
quality of courts, protection of property rights, copyright violations and constraints
to exercise "voice" of the firm. Bribery is expressed as percentage of revenues.
Fixed country effects were used for all countries, except for Latvia (benchmark) to
account for differences across individual countries. World averages were used for
some variables in those countries that were entirely missing observations for that
specific variable, in order to maximize the efficiency of estimators without affecting
their lack of bias. All firm characteristics are defined as a binary choice.
Source: Kaufmann, Mastruzzi, and Zavaleta (forthcoming).

cant, implying that, controlling for other factors, a firm's age, sector, or
mode of ownership do not influence its underreporting of revenue.

The prevalence of corruption matters enormously in a firm's behavior
and performance, yet analysis of WBES data suggests that the unpredictability of bribery or corruption does not matter significantly, controlling for the corruption level. This helps to resolve a source of debate in
development literature. Although, in general, the literature treating corruption presents it as a negative factor in development (Rose-Ackerman
1978, Klitgaard 1988, Shleifer and Vishny 1994, Mauro 1997), some authors claim it is the unpredictability of its costs, rather than the existence
or level of corruption, that discourages development. In other words, in
settings in which corruption is predictable, the premise is that corruption
would not have harmful effects compared to settings in which the degree
of unpredictability of corruption is much higher (Campos, Lien, and
Pradhan 1999).

Box 4.1 Controlling for Perception Bias—
The Kvetch Factor: Addressing Possible Errors in
Cross-Country Comparisons

In performing econometric work on the basis of survey data that contains an element of subjectivity or perception (as reflected in the nature of a firm's responses to the multiple questions applied during the interview), one challenge is that of possible spurious correlation between the dependent and independent variables: Firms that are doing well (by such performance measures as sales, which are often used as the dependent variables) may have rosier views of the obstacles to enterprises (which often are the independent variables) than would be warranted from an objective standpoint. Conversely, firms that perform poorly or that operate unofficially may exaggerate their accounts of their obstacles or be overly critical in their assessments of the effectiveness of government policies and services.

A particular firm's propensity to view all questions through the same subjective lens, creating a potentially spurious correlation between dependent and independent variables, has been called the "kvetch factor," after the Yiddish word for continually griping or complaining. If these variables are indeed affected by some unobservable but commonly perceived factor across variables by the same firm (such as the propensity to kvetch or its converse, a tendency to gloat throughout the survey interview), then this measurement error would lead coefficient estimates to be biased, and the likelihood of observing spurious correlations among variables whose true underlined correlation is insignificant cannot be ruled out.

To address this possible source of misspecification, Kaufmann and others (2001) first identified from the survey a number of possible kvetch control independent variables that fulfilled the condition of being a public good provided by the government that is commonly faced by all firms within a country.[18] Thus it can be presumed that the deviation of each firm's response from the country mean is a proxy for that firm's kvetch factor. Given that the firm-level econometric specifications they performed included country effects, direct inclusion of the universal public good suffices as proxy for the kvetch effect, as the subtraction from the country mean is implicitly taken care of by the country effect dummies.

Specifically, they identified four different kvetch control proxies, each inserted separately in a set of econometric specifications: extent of government efficiency, extent of helpfulness by government, quality of public works, and quality of the postal service. Because of their generic nature, the first two proxies we use in these tests have the advantage of being less subject to enormous variations across different locations (within a city), while the two variables of specific infrastructure nature are less subject to preferential provision, or exclusion, by the government to a firm. In the

(continued on next page)

Box 4.1, *continued*

unofficialdom analysis reported in table 4.3, this was done with two different variables from the same survey instrument: the degree of government
inefficiency as perceived by the firm and the firm's view on how helpful
the government was to enterprise. Insofar as there is a significant kvetch
factor, it would be picked up by these variables. In all cases we find that inclusion of the control variables do not affect the magnitude or high significance of the other variables in the specifications.

These results were also replicated with the other two kvetch control
variables (not shown here); namely, quality of public works and of postal
services, and also in these cases the magnitude and significance of the explanatory variables were not altered by inclusion of alternative kvetch control variables. Second, as an additional test, we also performed a two-stage
procedure to purge the possible kvetch bias from all independent variables: first we regressed each individual explanatory variable on a kvetch
control variable (inefficiency of government). The residuals of each regression were then used in the second stage to determine the effect of these
residual variables on the dependent variable, namely underreported revenues. Thus, while we found some evidence that some degree of a kvetch
factor may be at play (particularly in the cases of efficiency of government
and quality of public works as proxies, whose coefficients are significant),
we did not find evidence suggesting that the kvetch factor is a source of
misspecification and bias of the estimates for the explanatory variables.

Predictability of corruption is characterized by the bribe payer and re-
ceiver both knowing "what it takes" in terms of the nature and amount of
payment required, and the degree of certainty on the part of the payer
that the privately purchased "service" will actually be delivered by the
official. The premise is that in settings in which corruption is predictable,
corruption would have fewer harmful effects; it is, quite literally, business
as usual. However, in settings in which the degree of unpredictability of
corruption is much higher, the effects of corruption would be much more
harmful.

The WBES firm-level dataset permits an empirical evaluation of the
"unpredictability of corruption" hypothesis. We tested it using three separate variables derived from responses to the WBES. One indicated uncertainty about the price of corrupt services; one indicated uncertainty
about whether other officials might subsequently request additional bribe
payments; and one indicated uncertainty about whether bribes would result in the actual delivery of purchased services. As reported in table 4.4,
we found that, controlling for other factors, there is no significant rela-

Table 4.4 Underreported Revenues Versus Unpredictability of Corruption

Determinant	Estimate (t statistic)					
	1	2	3	4	5	6
Business constraints						
Financing	−0.04	0.42	0.30	0.11	−0.12	0.24
	(−0.11)	(1.16)	(0.67)	(0.26)	(−0.30)	(0.67)
Inflation	−0.15	−0.12	−0.31	−0.09	0.03	−0.04
	(−0.52)	(−0.49)	(−0.99)	(−0.32)	(0.10)	(−0.18)
Policy instability	0.77	0.74	0.82	0.58	0.51	0.55
	(2.76***)	(2.94***)	(2.71***)	(2.05**)	(1.90*)	(2.23**)
Infrastructure	0.89	0.68	0.80	0.39	0.42	0.22
	(2.07**)	(1.72+)	(1.75*)	(0.91)	(1.04)	(0.59)
Tax/regulatory	1.30	1.25	1.40	0.73	0.76	0.80
	(2.44**)	(2.72***)	(2.50**)	(1.39)	(1.51+)	(1.78*)
Unpredictability of corruption						
Bribery (percentage	0.28	0.29	0.27	—	—	—
of revenues)	(4.68***)	(4.91***)	(4.38***)	—	—	—
Frequency of bribing	—	—	—	2.16	1.84	2.01
				(6.90***)	(6.23***)	(8.07***)
Corrupt service	—	—	−0.01	0.44	—	—
unpredictability	—	—	(−0.03)	(1.51+)	—	—
Corrupt payment	0.01	—	—	—	0.26	—
unpredictability	(0.03)	—	—	—	(0.95)	—
Corrupt extra request	—	−0.10	—	—	—	0.10
unpredictability	—	(−0.37)	—	—	—	(0.40)
Government inefficiency	—	—	—	1.30	1.39	1.05
	—	—	—	(3.28***)	(3.59***)	(3.01***)
Firm characteristics						
Private ownership	−0.44	0.10	−0.11	0.05	−0.97	−0.44
	(−0.32)	(0.08)	(−0.07)	(0.04)	(−0.75)	(−0.36)
Small firm	4.42	4.94	5.23	5.50	4.60	4.75
	(3.43***)	(4.49***)	(3.63***)	(4.06***)	(3.71***)	(4.40***)
Medium-size firm	0.84	0.97	2.01	2.26	1.18	0.89
	(0.73)	(0.98)	(1.54+)	(1.84*)	(1.06)	(0.92)
Newer firm (started	−0.23	0.19	−0.20	0.09	0.04	0.36
since 1994)	(−0.36)	(0.35)	(−0.31)	(0.15)	(0.07)	(0.67)
Exporter	−0.89	−1.30	−1.59	−1.22	−0.53	−1.18
	(−0.97)	(−1.60+)	(−1.57+)	(−1.29)	(−0.61)	(−1.49+)
Foreign investment	−3.64	−3.37	−3.88	−3.07	−2.81	−2.92
	(−3.42***)	(−3.69***)	(−3.24***)	(−2.75***)	(−2.76***)	(−3.26***)
Location, small city	−0.13	0.18	−0.17	−0.01	0.00	0.01
	(−0.11)	(0.16)	(−0.13)	(−0.01)	(0.00)	(0.01)

(continued on next page)

Table 4.4, *continued*

Determinant	Estimate (t statistic)					
	1	2	3	4	5	6
Location, large city	1.42	2.18	1.38	1.24	1.29	1.53
	(1.36)	*(2.26**)*	*(1.25)*	*(1.20)*	*(1.31)*	*(1.65+)*
Manufacturing	1.81	1.94	1.97	1.74	1.82	2.04
	(0.85)	*(0.93)*	*(0.69)*	*(0.62)*	*(0.83)*	*(0.95)*
Service	0.34	0.38	0.24	0.67	1.05	1.14
	(0.13)	*(0.16)*	*(0.08)*	*(0.22)*	*(0.42)*	*(0.46)*
Agriculture	–0.64	–0.04	–0.63	0.18	0.50	0.66
	(–0.30)	*(–0.02)*	*(–0.22)*	*(0.07)*	*(0.23)*	*(0.31)*
Construction	1.39	1.70	1.62	1.63	1.73	1.73
	(0.60)	*(0.77)*	*(0.54)*	*(0.56)*	*(0.74)*	*(0.75)*
Adjusted R^2	0.19	0.19	0.19	0.18	0.17	0.20
Number of observations	3,262	3,902	2,926	3,347	3,369	4,223

***Significant at 1 percent; **significant at 5 percent; *significant at 10 percent; +significant at 15 percent.
— Variable not used in this equation.
a. Large firms constitute the benchmark.
b. Location in capital constitutes the benchmark.
c. Other sectors constitute the benchmark.
Note: From the survey, business constraints were rated on a scale from 1 to 4, where 1 implies "no constraint" and 4 implies a "major obstacle." These include inflation, financing, infrastructure, tax/regulation, and policy instability constraints, as well as quality of courts, protection of property rights, copyright violations and constraints to exercise "voice" of the firm. Bribery is expressed as percentage of revenues. Although not reported in the table, fixed country effects were used to account for differences across individual countries. World averages were used for some variables in those countries that were entirely missing observations for that specific variable, in order to maximize the efficiency of estimators without affecting their lack of bias. Finally, all firm characteristics are defined as a binary choice.
Source: Kaufmann, Mastruzzi, and Zavaleta (forthcoming).

tionship between *the degree of unpredictability* of corruption and the degree of underreporting of revenues by the firm. By contrast, the magnitude and significance of *the level of corruption* variables (proxied by the amounts of bribes paid or by the frequency of bribery) remain very high. These results occur regardless of which (and if any) of the three "unpredictability of corruption" components is used in our econometric specifications.

Referring to table 4.2, we also find results similar to those reported in table 4.1 in terms of which firm characteristics matter, controlling for other factors. Firms that are not large (small or medium-size), produce for the domestic market (nonexporters), lack foreign investment, and are privately owned tend to engage more in unofficial activity. By contrast, the coefficients for both de novo firms and for location are insignificant, implying that, controlling for other factors, neither the firm's age nor its location of headquarters is a determinant.

Severity of Constraints and Firm Characteristics: Size Matters in Complex Ways

The details of the WBES dataset permit an investigation of how a variety of firm characteristics, such as size and type of ownership, affect their experiences and perceptions of constraints. For example, the data allow an investigation of whether the implicit "tax" imposed by inappropriate government policies and regulations is evenly or unevenly distributed across different types of firms within a country. To do so, the authors analyzed the influence of firm characteristics on their responses to key potential obstacles to business operation and growth, using a multivariate regression approach to control for country effects.

An econometric review of the many key potential obstacles to business suggests that firms that are private, smaller, and newer; that have foreign direct investment (FDI); and that cater to the domestic market generally tend to face more acute business constraints than firms that are state-owned, older, and larger; export goods; and have FDI. (Probit models for the different constraints are estimated using firm characteristics as explanatory variables.)

There were some notable exceptions regarding some business constraints, however. For example, older firms reported being more constrained by political instability than younger firms and exporters were hit harder by inflation than nonexporters (see table 4.5).

In terms of firm size, globally on average, small and medium-size firms reported being more constrained than large firms along most dimensions (Schiffer and Weder 2001). Within small and medium enterprises, small firms are generally more constrained than medium-size firms. This may be either because the objective conditions of relatively larger firms are better or because they can better cope with constraints. For a more in-depth analysis of size effects, see Schiffer and Weder.

The analysis of firm characteristics allows a subtle reading of the data shown in table 4.5. For example, corruption is perceived as more constraining by smaller and younger firms, but also by those with government or public ownership and those that export. An inadequate exchange rate regime appears to be felt more by medium-size firms, younger firms, and those with some state ownership.

Table 4.5 Results of Least-Square Estimates: Obstacle Severity by Firm Characteristics

Dependent variable	Explanatory variables/Estimate (t statistic)							
	Small firm	Medium-size firm	Firm with foreign ownership	Firm with government control	Firm that exports	Firm located in a large city	Firm located in a small city	N
Finance	0.22***	0.16***	−0.33***	0.11***	0.07***	0.02	0.06	9,211.00
	(−6.53)	(−5.13)	(−10.97)	(−2.92)	(−2.60)	(−0.72)	(−1.62)	
Taxes and regulations	0.07***	0.08***	−0.10***	−0.17***	0.01	0.00	0.02	9,384.00
	(−2.73)	(−3.08)	(−3.84)	(−5.83)	(−0.24)	(−0.08)	(−0.64)	
Inflation	0.17***	0.10***	−0.08***	−0.08**	−0.05**	−0.03	0.01	9,111.00
	(−5.77)	(−3.556)	(−3.11)	(−2.38)	(−2.41)	(−1.19)	(−0.37)	
Exchange rate	0.09***	0.03	0.06*	−0.11***	0.12***	0.02	0.09***	8,990.00
	(−2.70)	(−0.97)	(−2.07)	(−3.00)	(−4.64)	(−0.72)	(−2.62)	
Corruption	0.21***	0.11***	−0.05*	−0.17***	0.00	0.02	0.03	8,359.00
	(−6.03)	(−3.61)	(−1.74)	(−4.46)	(−0.12)	(−0.52)	(−0.81)	
Tax administration	0.05*	0.06**	−0.07**	−0.18***	0.01	0.01	0.07**	9,479.00
	(−1.66)	(−2.17)	(−2.04)	(−5.15)	(−0.52)	(−0.39)	(−2.22)	
Infrastructure	−0.08***	−0.02	0.01	−0.13***	−0.02	0.02	0.05	9,119.00
	(−2.56)	(−0.76)	(−0.25)	(−3.88)	(−0.78)	(−0.70)	(−1.47)	
Policy instability	0.04	0.04	−0.02	−0.11***	0.01	−0.03	0.00	9,016.00
	(−1.28)	(−1.03)	(−0.62)	(−3.32)	(−0.52)	(−1.18)	(−0.13)	
High taxes	0.07***	0.09***	−0.09***	−0.24***	0.00	0.02	0.03	9,695.00
	(−2.74)	(−2.93)	(−3.58)	(−7.68)	(−0.19)	(−0.65)	(−0.97)	
Street crime	0.19***	0.07**	−0.08***	−0.11***	−0.08***	0.00	−0.02	8,801.00
	(−5.70)	(−2.47)	(−2.66)	(−3.11)	(−3.21)	(−0.10)	(−0.47)	
Bribes as percentage of sales	0.25***	0.16***	−0.08	−0.26***	−0.08*	0.01	0.06	5,234.00
	(−4.31)	(−2.89)	(−1.54)	(−3.57)	(−1.79)	(−0.29)	(−0.98)	

***Significant at 1 percent; **significant at 5 percent; *significant at 10 percent.

84

Figure 4.1 Tax and Regulatory Constraint, by Size of Firm, WBES 2000

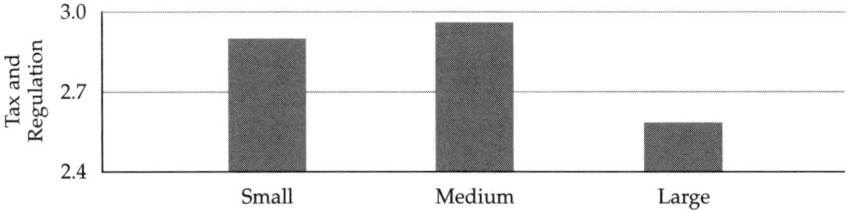

However, an exploration of the full results also gives rise to the notion of the forgotten middle. In facing some obstacles to doing business, medium-size firms identified themselves as equally or even more constrained than did small firms (see table 4.5 and figure 4.1). In particular, medium-size firms showed no statistical difference from small firms in their ratings of several general constraints and were significantly more likely to be seriously constrained by tax administration and infrastructure. With regard to infrastructure, large firms showed a statistically significant higher degree of constraint than medium-size and small firms.

These results suggest that policy interventions that unduly focus on very small or small enterprises may overlook important constraints to medium-size enterprises or all private enterprises. This may be related to a "threshold effect," where obstacles may not constrain entry so much as they deter firms' growth from small to medium size. As Brian Levy (1993) explains, "The threshold burden comprises a discontinuity in the structure of costs that results where some fiscal or bureaucratic burden is imposed only on firms above a minimum size. This discontinuity can lead some firms to rein in expansion—or to expand inefficiently by creating quasi-independent enterprises, each smaller than the threshold at which the tax and regulatory requirements are imposed."

In fact, the complexity characterizing the way in which different obstacles appear to affect different types of enterprises reinforces the rationale for focusing on across-the-board reduction of obstacles to business rather than the often unproductive earmarking of targeted policies according to firms' characteristics, such as size. To focus only on small firms would ignore the plight of mid-size firms. Even the preceding qualified generalizations require particular caution when we study a particular country or region.

Box 4.2 Firm Performance and State Capture in Transition—Using WBES to Unbundle Governance to Analyze the Firm's Role in Shaping the Business Environment

State capture, a form of grand corruption, was measured and analyzed for 22 transition economies in the transition Europe version of the WBES (the "BEEPS"). State capture is defined as the ability of firms to shape the laws, policies, and regulations of the state to their own advantage by providing illicit private gains to public officials. In transition economies, corruption has taken on a new image: that of so-called oligarchs or related elite enterprises manipulating policy formation and even shaping the emerging informal business rules to their own very substantial advantage. Some influential firms are business environment "makers"; less influential firms are business environment "takers." Although this form of grand corruption is increasingly being recognized as the most pernicious and intractable problem in the political economy of reform, few systematic efforts have been made to distinguish its causes and consequences from those of other forms of corruption.

The transition economy version of the WBES permitted an empirical assessment of the extent to which countries may have experienced good or poor governance in the formation and shaping of policies, laws, and regulations. By taking the average share of firms affected across six institutions—parliament, the executive, criminal courts, the civil courts, the central bank, and political parties—a state capture index for each country was developed. The evidence indicates that there is a very large gap between countries in which this form of corruption is a serious problem, which are called high-capture economies, and those in which it is seen as a relatively modest problem, called low-capture economies. Among the low-capture economies are the most reform-minded in the region. The high-capture group includes countries regarded as partial reformers in both political and economic terms; indeed, their political regimes tend to be characterized by a greater concentration of power and limitations on political competition. State capture also is negatively related to the level of civil liberties (see figure B4.1).

This version of the WBES also permitted the identification of firms that have paid bribes to influence the content of laws, rules, or regulations (the captor firms). As seen in figure B4.2, in high-capture economies' captor firms grow more than twice as fast as other firms, whereas in high-capture economies the overall enterprise sector grows at somewhat less than half the rate of firms in low-capture economies. Capture is therefore a large "tax" on noncaptor firms, but state capture provides the captor firms with substantial private gains. The data also suggest that once a country has

(continued on next page)

Box 4.2, *continued*

fallen into the trap of a capture economy, foreign direct investment can magnify the problem (Hellman and others 2000, and Hellman and Kaufmann 2001).

Figure B4.1 State Capture and Reform

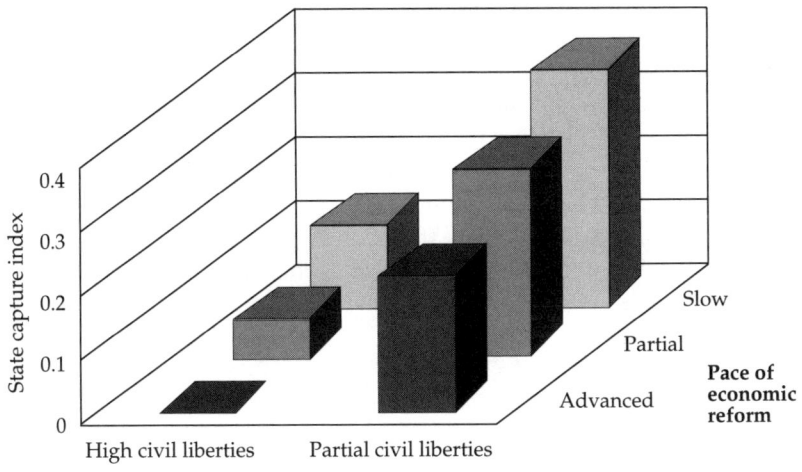

Figure B4.2 Private Benefits and Social Costs of State Capture

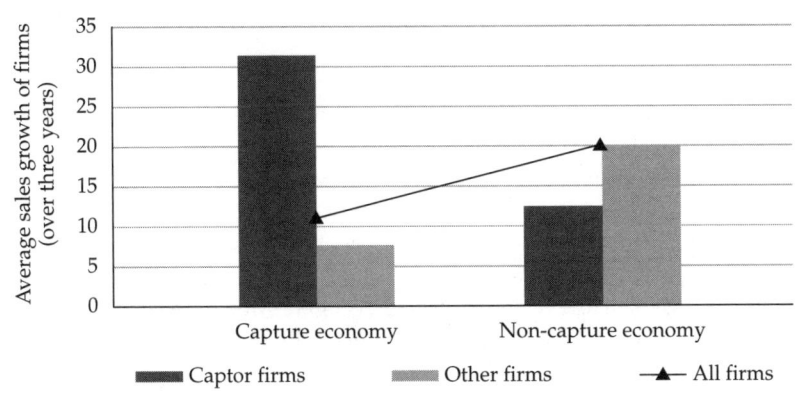

Annex:
Survey Questions for Variables Involved in Chapter Four

Underreported revenues: Recognizing the difficulties many enterprises face in fully complying with taxes and regulations, what percentage of total sales would you estimate the typical firm in your area of activity reports for tax purposes? (percentage)

Constraints in: Financing; Policy Instability; Exchange Rate; Inflation; Corruption; Tax/Regulations (for each): Please judge on a four-point scale how problematic are the following factors for the operation and growth of your business. [1, no obstacle; 4, major obstacle]

Bribery: On average, what percent of revenues do firms like yours typically pay per annum in unofficial payments to public officials? (percentage)

Availability of laws: In general, information on the laws and regulations affecting my firm is easy to obtain. [1, fully agree; 6, fully disagree]

Quality of services: Please rate the overall quality and efficiency of services delivered by the following public agencies or services (education, judiciary/courts, public works, postal system, water, police, central bank). [1, very good; 6, very bad]

Copyrights violations: Please judge on a four-point scale how problematic the following practices of your competitors are for your firm ("they violate my copyrights, patents or trademarks"). [1, no obstacle; 4, major obstacle]

Frequency of bribery: Thinking about government officials, it is common for firms in my line of business to have to pay some irregular additional payments to get things done. [1, always true; 6, never true]

Corrupt service unpredictability: If a firm pays the required additional payment the service is usually also delivered as agreed. [1, always true; 6, never true]

Corrupt payment unpredictability: Firms in my line of business usually know in advance about how much this additional payment is. [1, always true; 6, never true]

Corrupt extra payment unpredictability: If a firm pays the required additional payment to a particular government official, another government official will subsequently require an additional payment for the same service. [1, always true; 6, never true]

Government inefficiency: How would you generally rate the efficiency of government in delivering services? [1, very efficient; 6, very inefficient]

Government unhelpfulness: Please rate your overall perception of the relation between government and/or bureaucracy and private firms on the following scale. All in all, for doing business I perceive the state as: [1, very helpful; 5, very unhelpful]

5

Conclusions and Implications

The results of the World Business Environment Survey show that important dimensions in the climate for business operations and investment can be measured, analyzed, and compared across countries, and that important governance aspects are centrally related to the business environment. Further, the survey findings suggest that key policy, institutional, and governance indicators are connected to important outcomes, including sales by firms, investment growth, and the extent of unofficialdom. And they point to the value of monitoring such indicators over time, because progress in these areas should yield real improvements in enterprise performance.

In particular, the WBES provides empirical confirmation for some commonly held truths but provides little evidence for others. For example, it shows a clear connection between taxation, financing, and corruption on one hand, and growth and investment on the other. It suggests the importance of government consultation with key economic stakeholders as it attempts to provide an effective environment in which firms can grow, as well as the potential gains in investment from more stable economic policies. It suggests that weak investment climate conditions associated with macroeconomic instability, regulatory and tax constraints, and weak governance all play a role in unofficialdom and affect the size of the "shadow" economy.

At the same time, the WBES discourages generalizations about the global business environment. Rather, it sheds light on the enormous variance in the nature and severity of different types of constraints across countries and regions, as well as among firms of different characteristics. This variance implies that generalizations regarding the severity of a particular constraint are of limited value. It also suggests the importance of "unbundling" generic clusters of constraints. For example, although two countries may have severe regulatory or governance constraints, the components for each nation may be quite different. The detail afforded by the survey also suggests that generalizations about firm size and formality may benefit from a nuanced analysis of actual conditions. The country-specific data, initial analysis, and findings emerging from this report, as well as related papers and outputs from the WBES data (see the bibliography) point to the value of repeating the WBES in the future.

The complex interaction between firm size and the severity of reported constraints poses a challenge for policymakers who would target interventions to a single type of firm. The relationship between firm size and the severity of a constraint (with the smallest firms facing the most daunting constraints), while clearly there, is not equally strong for all constraints. Instead, for some constraints, medium-size firms show no difference from small ones; for several they are actually more constrained. If such findings are validated through further empirical studies, some implications will emerge. First, it would then be prudent to focus specifically on each particular constraint and the ways they affect firms of different sizes because, depending on the constraint, small, medium, (or large) firms may be affected most gravely. Second, these results would argue against policies targeted to small (or medium) enterprises, based on the notion that such policies are needed to level the playing field.

At the same time, this type of business survey paves the way toward a deeper understanding of a firm's behavior in shaping its business environment and investment climate. A major finding of a research project associated with this survey effort was that, contrary to conventional wisdom, a firm should not be seen as merely a passive business and investment climate "taker," for which the government presumably is the primary source of all business constraints. Instead, the data from transition countries that permitted an in-depth analysis of "state capture" highlighted empirically the extent to which powerful firms play a key role in shaping the policies, laws, and regulations that form the business environment and investment climate. This data leads to the notion that some firms become business climate "makers," particularly in countries where state capture or other related forms of firm influence is prevalent. In these cases, the actions of selected firms in many countries contribute to the shaping of such governance and investment climate in the first place. The effect of a firm's strategy on the business climate through its (privately induced) effect on public misgovernance further illustrates how important it is to view both governance and the investment climate within an integrated framework.

The implementation of the WBES offered a few lessons that apply to similar future projects. First, because WBES was a multipartner venture, coordination by all participants on a core instrument and uniform implementation would have enhanced its reliability and comparability across many more variables. Second, it is important to account for inherent biases and measurement errors in any survey of this type. This necessitates care in interpretation and the use of control variables, as discussed in chapter four. Furthermore, it points to the need for complementing the results of a firm survey with other data rather than considering a single survey as the single source of data for an assessment of the investment climate.

Next, as the extensive use of country control variables and the discussion of "kvetch control" indicates, even though perceptions matter significantly for the firm's behavior and decisionmaking, they are only imperfectly related to underlying physical and cost conditions. This underscores the desirability, when possible, of complementing questions of perception with more quantitative evaluations of a firm's experience of costs associated with various constraints. The World Bank Group's current core investment climate survey moves in this direction.[19]

Furthermore, for the next survey of firms (already initiated in some countries), it will be important to obtain a larger sample size in each country (to lower the measurement error) and to ensure that implementation is comparable with the approach taken during WBES 2000. This is particularly true for economy-wide sampling, for replicating the core questions, and for ensuring a similar interview framework for gathering information on a firm's influence and response to the governance and policy environment.

Finally, the country-specific data, initial analysis, and findings emerging from the WBES in this paper and other empirical work (see the bibliography) points to the importance of measuring and monitoring business environment indicators over time. The relationship shown between key WBES indicators and firm-level outcomes suggests that progress in these business and governance indicators should be associated with real improvements in enterprise performance over extended periods. Now that this survey approach, involving such a large number of partnerships, has been implemented (roughly) simultaneously across so many regions and countries, it would be extremely valuable to institutionalize its implementation every three to five years.

Annex 1

WBES Core Survey: "Measuring Conditions for Business Operation and Growth"

Private Enterprise Questionnaire

The purpose of this survey is to better understand constraints that hinder the development of private businesses like yours. This study is being conducted for 100* countries by the World Bank and its partners on the World Business Environment Survey team. The ultimate goal of this research is to advise governments on ways to change policies that impose a burden on private firms and to develop new projects and programs that strengthen support for enterprise growth. Your answers should reflect only your perception and experience of doing business in your country.

Please note that the information obtained here will be treated strictly anonymously and confidentially. Neither your name nor the name of your firm will be used in any document based on this survey.

General Information

i. Country: _____

		Today	Three years ago
ii.	Company size: number of full-time employees:	_____	_____
	number of part-time employees:	_____	_____

iii. Year of start-up: _____

iv. Industry:

Manufacturing	[ ]
If manufacturing, garment firm?	[ ]
If manufacturing, agro-processing?	[ ]
If manufacturing, heavy industry? *(machine tools, chemicals, autos, etc.)*	[ ]
Services	[ ]
If services, tourism, hotel, restaurant?	[ ]
If services, transport and storage?	[ ]

*In reality, the WBES was carried out in only 80 countries and one territory (see table 1.1).

          If services, communications/information   [ ]
             technology?
          Commerce (*wholesale/retail trade*)   [ ]
          Agriculture, hunting, fishing and forestry [ ]
          Mining and quarrying   [ ]
          Electricity, gas, and water   [ ]
          Construction   [ ]

v.   Please specify your enterprise's leading products or services (*up to three*):

_____

vi. Location of management: Capital city   [ ]
                          Large city   [ ]
                          Small city or countryside   [ ]

vii. City name: _____

viii. Does any government agency or state body have a financial stake in the ownership of your firm?
     Yes [ ] (*specify percent of total ownership*) _____%   No [ ]

ix. Does any foreign company or individual have a financial stake in the ownership of your firm?
     Yes [ ] (*specify percent of total ownership and nationality percent of leading foreign owner*) _____
     No [ ]

x.   Does your firm export?
     Yes [ ] (*specify percent of total sales*) _____%   No [ ]

xi. Sales to state sector?
     Yes [ ] (*specify percent of total sales to state,*   No [ ]
              state agencies, or enterprises) _____%

xii. What is the legal organization of this company?
     Single proprietorship   [ ]
     Partnership   [ ]
     Cooperative   [ ]
     Corporation, privately held   [ ]
     Corporation listed on a stock exchange   [ ]
     Other (*specify*): _____ [ ]

xiii. Which of the following best describes the overall control of your firm, where control means making major decisions concerning the enterprise's direction? (*Allow only one choice.*)

"My firm is controlled by..."

		Today	*Three* *years ago*
(a)	individual owner(s)	1	1
(b)	a family	2	2
(c)	a domestic company group (conglomerate)	3	3
(d)	a foreign company or group	4	4
(e)	an investment fund or mutual fund	5	5
(f)	a bank	6	6
(g)	its board of directors/supervisory board	7	7
(h)	its managers	8	8
(i)	its workers	9	9
(j)	government	10	10
(k)	other (*specify*): _____	11	11

xiv. Does your firm have holdings or operations in other countries?
Yes [   ]   No [   ]

xv. If your firm has shareholders, what percent of your firm is held by the three largest shareholders, either directly or indirectly? _____%

xvi. How was your firm established (*circle one*)?
(a) Originally private, from time of start-up
(b) Privatization of a state-owned firm
(c) Private subsidiary of a formerly state-owned firm
(d) Joint venture, domestic and foreign private owners
(e) Other (*specify*): _____

I. QUALITY AND INTEGRITY OF PUBLIC SERVICES

1. Please rate the overall quality and efficiency of services delivered by the following public agencies or services: (If usual provider is private, N/A.)

		Very *good*	*Good*	*Slightly* *good*	*Slightly* *bad*	*Bad*	*Very* *bad*	
Regulatory/judicial								
(a)	Customs service/agency	1	2	3	4	5	6	N/A
(b)	The judiciary/courts	1	2	3	4	5	6	N/A
Infrastructure								
(c)	Roads department/public works	1	2	3	4	5	6	N/A
(d)	Postal service/agency	1	2	3	4	5	6	N/A
(e)	Telephone service/agency	1	2	3	4	5	6	N/A
(f)	Electric power company/agency	1	2	3	4	5	6	N/A
(g)	Water/sewerage agency	1	2	3	4	5	6	N/A

Human services
| (g) | Public health care service/ hospitals | 1 | 2 | 3 | 4 | 5 | 6 N/A |
| (h) | Education services/schools | 1 | 2 | 3 | 4 | 5 | 6 N/A |

Security
| (i) | Police | 1 | 2 | 3 | 4 | 5 | 6 N/A |
| (j) | Armed forces/military | 1 | 2 | 3 | 4 | 5 | 6 N/A |

Policy/legislation
(k)	Central government leadership (*president/PM/ cabinet*)	1	2	3	4	5	6 N/A
(l)	Regional government	1	2	3	4	5	6 N/A
(m)	The parliament	1	2	3	4	5	6 N/A
(n)	The central bank	1	2	3	4	5	6 N/A

2. Does your firm own a generator because of unreliable or fluctuating electric power supply? Yes [   ]   No [   ]

3. a. If you import, how long does it typically take from the time your goods arrive in their point of entry (e.g., port, airport) until the time you can claim them from customs? _____ days   N/A
   b. How many days does the preshipment inspection process take, from the time you submit the goods until the time they are released? a. for imports _____ days   b. for exports _____ days   N/A

4. Does your firm have Internet access? Yes [   ]   No [   ]

II. Rules and Regulations

5. "In general, information on the laws and regulations affecting my firm is easy to obtain." To what degree do you agree with this statement?
   (1) Fully agree
   (2) Agree in most cases
   (3) Tend to agree
   (4) Tend to disagree
   (5) Disagree in most cases
   (6) Fully disagree

6. "In general, interpretations of regulations affecting my firm are consistent and predictable." To what degree do you agree with this statement?

		Today	Three years ago
(1)	Fully agree	[ ]	[ ]
(2)	Agree in most cases	[ ]	[ ]

(3)	Tend to agree	[ ]	[ ]
(4)	Tend to disagree	[ ]	[ ]
(5)	Disagree in most cases	[ ]	[ ]
(6)	Fully disagree	[ ]	[ ]

7. Please judge on a four-point scale how problematic are these different regulatory areas for the operation and growth of your business. (Please do not select more than four obstacles as "major" [4].) Please circle the most important obstacle.

		No obstacle	Minor obstacle	Moderate obstacle	Major obstacle
(a)	Business licensing	1	2	3	4
(b)	Customs/foreign trade regulations in your country	1	2	3	4
(c)	Labor regulations	1	2	3	4
(d)	Foreign currency/exchange regulations	1	2	3	4
(e)	Environmental regulations	1	2	3	4
(f)	Fire, safety regulations	1	2	3	4
(g)	Tax regulations/administration	1	2	3	4
(h)	High taxes	1	2	3	4

8. How often does the government intervene in the following types of decisions by your firm?

		Always	Usually	Frequently	Sometimes	Seldom	Never
(a)	Investment	1	2	3	4	5	6
(b)	Employment	1	2	3	4	5	6
(c)	Sales	1	2	3	4	5	6
(d)	Pricing	1	2	3	4	5	6
(e)	Mergers/acquisitions	1	2	3	4	5	6
(f)	Dividends	1	2	3	4	5	6
(g)	Wages	1	2	3	4	5	6

9. Please rate your overall perception of the relation between government and/or bureaucracy and private firms on the following scale. "All in all, for doing business I perceive the state as ... "

	Central/national government					Local/regional government				
	Very helpful	Mildly helpful	Neutral	Mildly unhelpful	Very unhelpful	Very helpful	Mildly helpful	Neutral	Mildly unhelpful	Very unhelpful
Now	1	2	3	4	5	1	2	3	4	5
Three years ago	1	2	3	4	5	1	2	3	4	5

III. Legal System

10. In resolving business disputes, do you believe your country's court system to be...

		Always	Usually	Frequently	Sometimes	Seldom	Never
(a)	fair and impartial	1	2	3	4	5	6
(b)	honest/uncorrupt	1	2	3	4	5	6
(c)	quick	1	2	3	4	5	6
(d)	affordable	1	2	3	4	5	6
(e)	consistent	1	2	3	4	5	6
(f)	decisions enforced	1	2	3	4	5	6

11. "I am confident that the legal system will uphold my contract and property rights in business disputes." To what degree do you agree with this statement?

		Today	Three years ago
(1)	Fully agree	[ ]	[ ]
(2)	Agree in most cases	[ ]	[ ]
(3)	Tend to agree	[ ]	[ ]
(4)	Tend to disagree	[ ]	[ ]
(5)	Disagree in most cases	[ ]	[ ]
(6)	Fully disagree	[ ]	[ ]

IV. Bureaucratic Red Tape

12. What percentage of senior management's time per year is spent in dealing with government officials about the application and interpretation of laws and regulations? _____ %

13. "Thinking about government officials, it is common for firms in my line of business to have to pay some irregular 'additional payments' to get things done." This is true...
    (1) always
    (2) mostly
    (3) frequently
    (4) sometimes
    (5) seldom
    (6) never (skip to question 16)

14. "Firms in my line of business usually know in advance about how much this 'additional payment' is." This is true...
    (1) always
    (2) mostly
    (3) frequently

    (4) sometimes
    (5) seldom
    (6) never

15. "If a firm pays the required 'additional payment,' the service is usually also delivered as agreed." This is true...
    (1) always
    (2) mostly
    (3) frequently
    (4) sometimes
    (5) seldom
    (6) never

16. "If a firm pays the required additional payment to a particular government official, another government official will subsequently require an additional payment for the same service..."
    (1) always
    (2) mostly
    (3) frequently
    (4) sometimes
    (5) seldom
    (6) never

17. "If a government agent acts against the rules, I can usually go to another official or to his superior and get the correct treatment without recourse to unofficial payments." This is true...
    (1) always
    (2) mostly
    (3) frequently
    (4) sometimes
    (5) seldom
    (6) never

18. During the last year, please characterize the interactions you had in each of the following contexts.

	During the last year, how many times did your enterprise have contact with this agency or type of official?	*In what percent of these contacts did a public official indicate or request that you should make an extra payment?*	*On average, how much was required as payment (in equivalent value if it took the form of gift or other favor)?*
Electric power company	_____	_____ %	$ _____
Telephone company	_____	_____ %	$ _____
Business license authority	_____	_____ %	$ _____
Tax agency/ inspectors	_____	_____ %	$ _____
Government procurement agents	_____	_____ %	$ _____
Customs and trade licensing officials	_____	_____ %	$ _____
Judges/court officials	_____	_____ %	$ _____
Politicians influencing policies affecting your firm	_____	_____ %	$ _____
Other (*specify*):	_____	_____ %	$ _____

19. On average, what percent of revenues do firms like yours typically pay per annum in unofficial payments to public officials?

0%	1
Less than 1%	2
1–1.99%	3
2–9.99%	4
10–12%	5
13–25%	6
Over 25%	7
Don't know	8

20. When firms in your industry do business with the government, how much of the contract value must they offer in additional or unofficial payments to secure the contract?
    (1) 0%
    (2) Up to 5%
    (3) 6–10%
    (4) 11–15%
    (5) 16–20%
    (6) Greater than 20% (*specify* _____ %)
    DK Don't know

21. When a new law, rule, regulation, or decree is being discussed that could have a substantial impact on your business, how much influence does your firm typically have at the national level of government on the content of that law, rule, regulation, or decree?

	1 = Never influential	2 = Seldom influential	3 = Influential	4 = Frequently influential	5 = Very influential
Executive	[ ]	[ ]	[ ]	[ ]	[ ]
Legislature	[ ]	[ ]	[ ]	[ ]	[ ]
Ministry	[ ]	[ ]	[ ]	[ ]	[ ]
Regulatory agency	[ ]	[ ]	[ ]	[ ]	[ ]

V. PREDICTABILITY

22. Do you regularly have to cope with unexpected changes in economic and financial policies that materially affect your business? Changes in economic and financial policies are…
    (1) completely predictable
    (2) highly predictable
    (3) fairly predictable
    (4) fairly unpredictable
    (5) highly unpredictable
    (6) completely unpredictable

23. Do you regularly have to cope with unexpected changes in rules, laws, or regulations that materially affect your business? Changes in rules, laws, and regulations are...
    (1) completely predictable
    (2) highly predictable
    (3) fairly predictable
    (4) fairly unpredictable
    (5) highly unpredictable
    (6) completely unpredictable

24. Please evaluate the following statement: "The process of developing new rules, regulations, or policies is usually such that businesses are informed in advance of changes affecting them." This is true...
    (1) always
    (2) mostly
    (3) frequently
    (4) sometimes
    (5) seldom
    (6) never

25. "In case of important changes in laws or policies affecting my business operation, the government takes into account concerns voiced either by me or by my business association." This is true...
    (1) always
    (2) mostly
    (3) frequently
    (4) sometimes
    (5) seldom
    (6) never

26. "In the last three years, the laws, regulations and policies affecting my business have become..."
    (1) much more predictable
    (2) somewhat more predictable
    (3) unchanged
    (4) somewhat less predictable
    (5) much less predictable
    (6) don't know

VI. Financial Sector Services and Corporate Governance

27. "I have full confidence in the ability of my country's financial system to provide financing to private firms like mine." To what degree do you agree with this statement?

		Today	Three years ago
(1)	Fully agree	[ ]	[ ]
(2)	Agree in most cases	[ ]	[ ]
(3)	Tend to agree	[ ]	[ ]
(4)	Tend to disagree	[ ]	[ ]
(5)	Disagree in most cases	[ ]	[ ]
(6)	Fully disagree	[ ]	[ ]

28. Please identify the share (percentage) of your firm's fixed investment over the last year coming from each of the following sources:

Internal funds/retained earnings	_____ %
Equity, sale of stock	_____ %
Local commercial banks	_____ %
Investment funds/special development finance	_____ %
Other state sources	_____ %
Foreign banks	_____ %
Family/friends	_____ %
Money lenders, traditional or informal sources	_____ %
Supplier credit	_____ %
Leasing arrangement	_____ %
Other (specify): _____	_____ %
	100%

29. How long does it take to transfer money to a supplier through the financial system?
    (a) Domestic supplier   _____ days (now)
                                        _____ days (three years ago)
    (b) Foreign supplier   _____ days (now)
                                        _____ days (three years ago)

30. Please judge on a four-point scale how problematic are these different financing issues for the operation and growth of your business. (Please do not select more than four as "major obstacles" [4].) Please circle the most important.

		No obstacle	Minor obstacle	Moderate obstacle	Major obstacle
(a)	Collateral requirements of banks/ financial institutions	1	2	3	4
(b)	Bank paperwork/bureaucracy	1	2	3	4

(c)	High interest rates	1	2	3	4
(d)	Need special connections with banks/financial institutions	1	2	3	4
(e)	Banks lack money to lend	1	2	3	4
(f)	Lack access to long-term loans	1	2	3	4
(g)	Corruption of bank officials	1	2	3	4
(h)	Lack access to foreign banks	1	2	3	4
(i)	Lack access to nonbank equity/ investors/partners	1	2	3	4
(j)	Lack access to specialized export finance	1	2	3	4
(k)	Lack access to lease finance for equipment	1	2	3	4
(l)	Inadequate credit/financial information on customers	1	2	3	4

31. Does your firm use international accounting standards (IAS)?
    Yes [　]　No [　]

32. Does your firm provide its shareholders with annual financial statements that have been reviewed by an external auditor?
    Yes [　]　No [　]

VII. COMPETITION

33. Regarding your firm's major product line, how many competitors do you face in your markets?
    (a) none　(b) three or fewer　(c) many (*more than three*)

34. Which of the following would you define as your leading competitor?
    (a)　Domestic small and medium-size enterprises　　　　　1
    (b)　Domestic large private enterprises　　　　　　　　　2
    (c)　Foreign firm producing in domestic market (not imports)　3
    (d)　State-owned enterprises　　　　　　　　　　　　　4
    (e)　Micro-enterprises/informal sector　　　　　　　　　5
    (f)　Legal imports　　　　　　　　　　　　　　　　　6
    (g)　Smuggled goods　　　　　　　　　　　　　　　　7
    (h)　My firm has no competitors　　　　　　　　　　　　8
    (i)　Other (*specify*):_____　　　　　　　　9

35. Please judge on a four-point scale how problematic for your firm are the following practices of your competitors.

		No obstacle	Minor obstacle	Moderate obstacle	Major obstacle
(a)	They avoid sales tax, VAT, or other taxes.	1	2	3	4
(b)	They do not pay duties or observe trade regulations.	1	2	3	4
(c)	Foreign producers sell below international prices.	1	2	3	4
(d)	Domestic producers unfairly sell below my prices.	1	2	3	4
(e)	They avoid labor taxes/regulations (e.g., social security).	1	2	3	4
(f)	They violate my copyrights, patents, or trademarks.	1	2	3	4
(g)	They receive subsidies (including the toleration of tax arrears) from national/local government.	1	2	3	4
(h)	They have favored access to credit, infrastructure services, or customers.	1	2	3	4

36. Recognizing the difficulties many enterprises face in fully complying with taxes and regulations, what percentage of total sales would you estimate the typical firm in your area of activity reports for tax purposes?

(a)	All (100%)	1
(b)	90–99%	2
(c)	80–89%	3
(d)	70–79%	4
(e)	60–69%	5
(f)	50–59%	6
(g)	Less than 50% (*specify* _____%)	7

VIII. SUMMARY QUESTIONS

37. How would you generally rate the efficiency of government in delivering services?

		Today	Three years ago
(1)	Very efficient	[ ]	[ ]
(2)	Efficient	[ ]	[ ]
(3)	Mostly efficient	[ ]	[ ]
(4)	Mostly inefficient	[ ]	[ ]
(5)	Inefficient	[ ]	[ ]
(6)	Very inefficient	[ ]	[ ]

38. Please judge on a four-point scale how problematic are the following factors for the operation and growth of your business. (Please do not select more than three obstacles as "major" [4].) Please circle the most important obstacle:

		No obstacle	Minor obstacle	Moderate obstacle	Major obstacle
(a)	Financing	1	2	3	4
(b)	Infrastructure (e.g., telephone, electricity, water, roads, land)	1	2	3	4
(c)	Taxes and regulations	1	2	3	4
(d)	Policy instability/uncertainty	1	2	3	4
(e)	Inflation	1	2	3	4
(f)	Exchange rate	1	2	3	4
(g)	Functioning of the judiciary	1	2	3	4
(h)	Corruption	1	2	3	4
(i)	Street crime/theft/disorder	1	2	3	4
(j)	Organized crime/mafia	1	2	3	4
(k)	Anticompetitive practices by government or private enterprises	1	2	3	4
(l)	Other (specify):_____	1	2	3	4

IX. ECONOMIC PERFORMANCE

39. Please estimate the growth of your company's sales, investment, exports, employment, and debt over the past year.

	Sales ($ value)	Investment ($ value)	Exports ($ value)	Full-time employment (# workers)	Debt ($ value)
Increase	___%	___%	___%	___%	___%
No change	0	0	0	0	0
Decline	___%	___%	___%	___%	___%

40. Please predict the growth of your company's sales, investment, and employment over the next year.

	Sales ($ value)	Investment ($ value)	Exports ($ value)	Full-time employment (# workers)	Debt ($ value)
Increase	___%	___%	___%	___%	___%
No change	0	0	0	0	0
Decline	___%	___%	___%	___%	___%

41. For background purposes only (to compare your firm to others in our
    sample), please estimate
    (a) the value of your firm's total sales in the last one year:
         $_____
    (b) the value of your firm's fixed assets (land, building, equipment):
         $_____
    (c) the value of your firm's debts:
         $_____

Thank you very much for having taken the time to complete this questionnaire. The information on your perceptions is a very important input
for the evaluation of conditions in the business environment and private
sector relations with government, as well as for the formulation of policy
advice.

  We would appreciate any thoughts you might like to add on the business environment, on the relationship between the private sector and
government, or comments on the questionnaire in general.

THE SURVEY ENDS HERE.
THANK YOU FOR YOUR COOPERATION.

Annex 2

WBES World Tables

Country Responses to Key WBES Questions

Caution: Given inherent error margins associated with any single survey result, it is inappropriate to use the results from this survey for precise country rankings in any particular dimension of the investment climate or governance.

Table A2.1 General Constraints to Operation and Growth

Economy	Corruption	Judiciary	Financing	Infrastructure	Policy instability	Inflation	Exchange rate	Street crime	Organized crime	Anti-competitive policies	Taxes and regulations
Eastern Europe and Central Asia											
Albania	82.05	53.28	63.58	75.16	87.04	57.41	50.00	87.42	82.58	52.14	73.46
Armenia	27.10	11.70	60.68	20.00	68.55	68.55	66.13	24.32	16.50	28.18	91.20
Azerbaijan	57.02	46.02	66.14	33.60	37.50	50.79	40.80	34.17	46.67	57.14	64.29
Belarus	22.94	11.54	82.79	22.76	67.57	93.55	73.50	33.04	21.70	25.93	85.48
Bosnia and Herzegovina	52.38	49.48	76.70	55.88	80.58	8.25	7.22	17.05	24.68	54.74	80.00
Bulgaria	54.78	42.02	73.33	43.55	71.31	59.20	48.72	57.98	51.69	49.06	77.42
Croatia	55.93	60.48	80.95	23.62	78.57	51.20	66.67	33.04	37.50	34.45	85.04
Czech Rep.	34.75	31.09	81.06	44.03	60.00	70.68	41.41	31.45	20.51	34.51	87.12
Estonia	21.77	15.52	53.79	17.42	53.49	43.51	26.23	35.66	18.90	20.83	59.85
Georgia	72.00	20.54	78.29	35.66	69.29	88.37	57.36	46.51	55.04	41.13	82.17
Hungary	28.10	9.43	61.42	15.75	58.87	55.56	17.12	25.21	22.81	38.39	75.59
Kazakhstan	52.13	26.32	79.53	38.10	63.56	92.13	84.80	50.86	41.90	50.51	80.65
Kyrgyz Rep.	82.98	35.90	87.20	33.88	85.71	96.77	88.14	82.61	74.19	72.04	91.87
Lithuania	53.06	36.26	69.81	24.55	50.00	56.36	28.97	53.85	48.45	49.47	82.14
Moldova	67.86	43.52	85.37	48.80	93.50	98.39	89.17	71.90	72.57	66.36	88.00
Poland	38.31	39.72	49.77	16.22	54.26	52.91	38.94	40.58	27.04	35.98	72.44
Romania	57.39	52.89	80.49	51.20	80.65	94.35	70.97	44.25	35.58	44.86	92.80
Russia	50.32	30.88	79.42	33.72	84.20	87.95	72.00	50.88	48.86	55.30	90.42
Slovak Rep.	45.45	37.90	83.72	28.57	18.02	73.64	47.90	51.22	45.00	36.59	79.84
Slovenia	15.57	44.80	45.60	18.40	50.40	30.40	35.20	13.82	14.63	42.28	64.00
Turkey	62.76	38.51	77.70	43.92	87.92	89.26	63.51	26.03	34.48	60.69	73.47
Ukraine	44.78	26.40	86.67	37.33	79.46	87.56	70.97	46.33	43.07	57.82	95.11
Uzbekistan	41.58	19.42	61.60	23.20	39.50	74.40	55.45	22.02	20.95	41.03	55.65

Latin America and the Caribbean

Argentina	52.04	42.86	70.00	22.00	73.74	31.31	26.32	47.96	31.25	51.58	86.00
Belize	30.00	17.02	55.10	30.00	38.00	31.25	18.37	39.58	18.18	32.61	54.00
Bolivia	88.66	61.86	71.72	54.00	73.00	51.00	45.00	59.00	40.63	54.74	75.00
Brazil	50.00	53.27	57.21	37.31	90.05	57.21	68.56	55.05	43.75	49.74	93.53
Chile	24.49	23.47	48.00	26.00	55.00	34.34	53.54	49.00	25.25	23.00	39.39
Colombia	59.00	42.00	55.00	49.49	87.13	68.32	81.00	76.24	71.29	38.14	79.00
Costa Rica	48.00	30.00	56.00	49.00	59.00	66.00	57.58	62.00	38.20	43.16	63.00
Dominican Rep.	69.72	49.09	54.95	54.05	68.47	63.96	62.73	73.87	64.86	55.45	71.17
Ecuador	87.88	76.53	81.44	54.84	88.89	95.00	93.00	85.71	71.13	51.35	78.79
El Salvador	70.30	57.43	65.05	54.37	71.84	75.73	56.31	92.23	91.09	44.90	78.64
Guatemala	51.96	46.08	64.76	49.06	74.29	82.08	89.62	76.19	65.71	37.62	62.26
Haiti	75.49	44.44	81.37	99.03	80.00	70.87	66.67	94.17	90.72	72.00	65.69
Honduras	58.62	37.18	70.97	42.39	44.44	81.72	75.00	76.34	48.75	62.22	62.64
Mexico	80.61	65.98	76.77	47.42	87.00	90.00	83.00	82.83	78.79	65.66	78.57
Nicaragua	59.57	38.95	72.45	60.20	64.95	86.46	75.26	59.79	42.53	50.52	72.45
Panama	64.65	51.55	36.36	42.00	63.00	34.34	13.95	70.71	57.58	52.04	49.00
Peru	62.14	47.06	74.29	38.68	75.47	60.75	71.70	65.05	40.59	60.40	83.02
Trinidad and Tobago	18.00	11.88	69.31	22.77	20.79	47.00	49.50	32.67	14.85	24.75	67.33
Uruguay	29.41	28.57	61.62	35.00	56.25	32.98	48.98	37.78	3.95	22.34	84.00
Venezuela, R.B. de	72.92	58.33	53.54	44.00	94.00	89.90	78.00	79.00	56.25	59.79	77.00

East Asia

Cambodia	n.a.	30.87	35.02	43.22	64.26	52.05	42.27	83.96	77.53	43.04	35.96
China	31.25	13.83	80.20	30.69	41.00	42.42	21.74	18.18	19.59	38.78	28.71
Indonesia	49.00	29.17	60.00	43.00	74.00	73.00	81.00	50.00	44.44	61.86	50.00
Malaysia	22.73	21.35	41.05	19.79	27.37	39.36	28.26	18.48	14.61	27.27	20.43
Philippines	73.00	38.38	57.00	64.00	69.00	87.00	83.00	64.00	52.58	66.00	72.00
Singapore	8.00	9.09	30.30	11.00	11.00	12.00	26.00	6.00	10.10	20.62	11.00
Thailand	87.06	25.00	75.24	64.89	90.85	90.59	94.77	92.59	100.00	95.40	84.25

(continued on next page)

111

Table A2.1, *continued*

Economy	Corruption	Judiciary	Financing	Infrastructure	Policy instability	Inflation	Exchange rate	Street crime	Organized crime	Anti-competitive policies	Taxes and regulations
Sub-Saharan Africa											
Botswana	10.71	n.a.	38.75	28.75	9.09	20.93	5.48	21.59	14.29	n.a.	0.00
Cameroon	92.68	n.a.	77.78	90.70	30.56	21.43	40.00	69.77	42.11	n.a.	66.67
Côte d'Ivoire	92.68	n.a.	72.37	42.86	72.50	48.05	27.14	89.02	26.47	n.a.	57.89
Ethiopia	45.71	n.a.	80.56	70.27	50.00	41.67	52.00	10.00	4.84	n.a.	23.81
Ghana	57.53	n.a.	80.52	57.97	32.86	89.61	47.83	38.89	47.06	n.a.	26.67
Kenya	90.10	n.a.	62.89	94.12	68.04	60.20	20.48	74.23	77.08	n.a.	28.57
Madagascar	87.62	n.a.	82.52	85.15	59.57	81.82	41.24	65.98	19.35	n.a.	47.62
Malawi	53.19	n.a.	63.27	89.36	27.91	93.75	44.44	68.75	95.00	n.a.	31.25
Namibia	9.20	n.a.	21.84	10.47	8.24	21.51	21.35	27.47	69.70	n.a.	8.33
Nigeria	87.72	n.a.	73.08	98.25	92.98	78.95	64.81	85.71	97.50	n.a.	25.00
Senegal	72.31	n.a.	72.58	78.13	43.10	50.00	32.76	52.46	32.73	n.a.	37.50
South Africa	50.47	n.a.	43.14	14.15	20.00	41.67	47.57	89.91	98.39	n.a.	20.00
Tanzania	68.66	n.a.	77.27	88.24	43.86	59.70	24.59	28.81	26.92	n.a.	50.00
Uganda	80.34	n.a.	73.73	70.00	49.57	53.33	16.82	44.35	69.77	n.a.	29.63
Zambia	60.56	n.a.	75.34	76.39	47.14	93.15	22.58	75.00	71.88	n.a.	33.33
Zimbabwe	69.52	n.a.	68.32	57.14	60.78	100.00	63.54	50.96	61.70	n.a.	62.50
OECD											
Canada	7.07	10.20	34.00	6.93	33.00	32.67	34.34	7.00	5.15	19.19	55.45
France	16.84	20.62	57.58	25.00	34.34	32.65	19.79	25.25	13.40	31.25	80.00
Germany	24.49	30.00	56.57	21.21	15.15	19.00	17.89	15.15	18.18	41.24	79.00
Italy	22.47	36.96	37.50	42.27	64.29	37.76	29.67	34.74	27.96	39.77	83.51
Portugal	15.46	10.20	17.53	18.37	25.51	42.27	11.46	11.46	5.38	43.30	31.31
Spain	38.54	33.67	40.20	26.73	47.00	43.43	27.78	26.53	19.57	42.86	60.40

Sweden	3.09	13.27	28.00	14.85	46.00	17.82	21.65	13.27	7.22	29.59	59.00
United Kingdom	5.26	13.86	41.58	16.67	37.25	36.27	45.26	29.59	12.12	16.00	63.73
United States	24.21	20.65	39.39	24.00	29.29	37.37	14.94	36.84	12.09	13.83	43.00
South Asia											
Bangladesh	91.67	51.28	54.35	n.a.	62.50	51.11	71.05	76.74	50.00	57.50	67.44
India	60.43	29.12	52.13	61.98	62.96	67.91	42.77	22.91	21.84	n.a.	39.23
Pakistan	83.00	52.53	83.17	77.45	91.09	74.26	71.00	63.27	64.95	57.14	80.39
MENA											
Egypt, Arab Rep. of	74.47	n.a.	85.11	76.60	77.78	70.21	73.81	62.22	20.83	n.a.	40.00
Tunisia	33.33	n.a.	11.90	19.44	19.05	14.71	20.93	11.54	0.00	n.a.	40.00
West Bank/Gaza	70.93	42.86	49.41	32.94	77.11	63.95	62.22	42.86	34.62	54.22	55.68
Total	51.12	35.12	63.47	41.42	61.76	62.20	51.85	49.61	41.89	45.57	69.53

n.a. Not asked in Africa and some MENA countries.
Note: Percentage of firms ranking the constraint as a "moderate" or "major" obstacle.

Table A2.2 Tax and Regulatory Constraints

Economy	Business registration	Customs	Labor	Foreign currency	Environmental	Fire	High taxes	Tax administration
Eastern Europe and Central Asia								
Albania	13.21	45.83	11.88	27.27	23.08	14.56	76.13	51.57
Armenia	21.60	28.80	3.20	27.42	19.20	5.60	88.80	73.60
Azerbaijan	25.20	35.65	30.65	32.28	29.92	32.28	77.34	53.91
Belarus	44.63	29.79	16.26	50.00	22.22	23.77	91.94	76.00
Bosnia and Herzegovina	31.91	35.48	49.48	36.56	32.22	20.88	78.57	66.67
Bulgaria	32.74	25.56	33.06	14.55	23.85	18.03	81.15	62.90
Croatia	25.20	32.48	33.33	28.46	35.25	32.00	95.28	70.87
Czech Rep.	26.87	34.62	43.41	32.23	33.08	32.59	89.63	81.62
Estonia	11.02	16.24	14.50	1.65	21.31	15.50	62.79	46.51
Georgia	35.94	35.09	26.56	14.17	28.57	22.48	92.25	74.22
Hungary	37.50	22.55	33.33	13.13	27.35	19.83	86.82	65.12
Kazakhstan	39.64	39.60	15.20	21.51	24.79	19.67	88.71	69.29
Kyrgyz Rep.	29.91	57.97	8.47	20.00	10.89	10.00	96.80	79.51
Lithuania	47.06	35.90	43.24	5.15	26.73	25.45	91.07	76.58
Moldova	50.41	37.93	17.21	17.65	23.21	19.51	91.20	80.00
Poland	8.68	37.43	47.27	22.51	31.10	27.15	83.33	68.75
Romania	26.02	45.33	24.39	33.00	16.95	9.02	94.35	69.60
Russia	42.97	29.13	18.76	24.23	29.98	26.11	92.32	79.19
Slovak Rep.	30.77	35.78	24.81	18.18	32.52	27.13	74.80	66.41
Slovenia	16.39	24.00	47.20	20.97	26.40	16.80	78.40	56.00
Turkey	18.79	25.69	33.78	16.33	33.56	18.92	82.64	66.89
Ukraine	44.19	47.22	23.98	43.02	33.18	30.36	95.56	86.10
Uzbekistan	28.57	39.42	14.88	51.55	22.76	12.00	70.16	50.40

Latin America and the Caribbean

Argentina	51.65	43.84	8.99	35.79	28.57	91.92	78.57
Belize	16.33	33.33	65.31	18.37	18.75	65.31	44.00
Bolivia	71.00	76.84	20.41	52.13	24.44	86.00	72.00
Brazil	61.93	59.02	51.08	47.21	37.24	97.51	87.50
Chile	44.79	29.79	19.19	58.51	27.84	59.38	40.40
Colombia	61.00	66.30	43.30	56.25	28.42	93.00	63.37
Costa Rica	62.50	56.52	13.13	39.80	16.16	78.35	49.48
Dominican Rep.	30.63	50.47	32.11	27.52	29.36	82.24	55.14
Ecuador	68.04	65.12	60.42	33.68	29.47	87.00	70.71
El Salvador	59.80	53.06	25.00	41.00	28.00	75.49	58.25
Guatemala	62.26	72.45	36.54	38.24	19.19	82.86	59.43
Haiti	30.00	50.00	48.00	16.13	17.89	79.80	57.43
Honduras	69.39	57.14	56.99	48.42	44.09	80.85	64.21
Mexico	78.57	63.22	40.21	55.43	53.06	89.90	74.49
Nicaragua	52.04	48.86	32.99	24.21	22.68	83.51	58.16
Panama	50.52	54.35	22.50	40.63	34.38	69.39	54.08
Peru	64.15	48.31	20.20	31.91	22.45	88.68	62.26
Trinidad and Tobago	33.00	51.49	29.70	17.82	22.77	72.28	49.50
Uruguay	35.16	53.61	5.15	19.35	21.65	92.00	53.06
Venezuela, R.B. de	77.32	68.42	27.84	24.49	30.61	77.55	64.65

East Asia

Cambodia	22.26	17.20	17.19	8.15	20.87	68.01	34.47
China	27.72	21.05	14.63	19.79	14.43	50.00	30.00
Indonesia	42.00	35.14	44.90	30.30	44.00	66.29	55.00
Malaysia	27.55	29.89	29.67	26.88	17.53	36.17	20.83
Philippines	33.67	48.96	53.54	43.43	24.24	75.76	54.55
Singapore	9.28	10.75	9.28	5.10	5.00	31.96	12.00
Thailand	26.92	47.64	53.98	42.07	33.73	80.91	69.93

(continued on next page)

Table A2.2, *continued*

Economy	Business registration	Customs	Labor	Foreign currency	Environmental	Fire	High taxes	Tax administration
Sub-Saharan Africa								
Botswana	14.58	11.70	26.04	2.13	9.89	9.89	13.83	10.98
Cameroon	30.61	66.00	46.94	44.90	26.53	19.57	88.89	81.40
Côte d'Ivoire	26.44	66.28	32.14	32.18	18.39	13.95	87.50	71.25
Ethiopia	10.11	55.56	17.05	49.47	8.00	5.13	70.65	64.94
Ghana	23.30	39.58	28.87	42.57	33.33	25.25	63.81	51.35
Kenya	44.55	54.00	33.66	15.53	19.19	9.18	83.02	56.25
Madagascar	23.42	63.55	18.39	44.14	29.36	15.60	91.89	86.67
Malawi	9.26	52.83	19.23	47.17	16.67	6.12	84.31	59.18
Namibia	8.70	18.68	52.22	20.00	9.78	3.33	62.92	25.84
Nigeria	37.04	73.75	24.36	60.76	41.98	32.91	70.73	47.27
Senegal	44.44	48.96	50.00	40.70	27.85	41.25	76.84	65.71
South Africa	15.25	21.85	84.87	43.97	17.39	7.76	71.79	47.17
Tanzania	46.15	66.20	54.05	23.94	31.94	24.29	91.14	78.87
Uganda	20.16	48.33	13.79	18.18	27.73	15.93	85.94	72.17
Zambia	22.08	40.26	39.47	19.23	18.42	25.00	85.90	66.67
Zimbabwe	33.33	66.67	56.30	71.31	12.07	7.69	92.62	66.67
OECD								
Canada	27.27	34.78	20.41	22.34	22.34	11.34	70.10	51.55
France	52.63	34.88	55.56	31.11	30.11	28.57	89.69	73.96
Germany	38.10	37.84	61.00	25.93	52.58	44.00	84.85	79.00
Italy	54.55	35.29	70.10	23.19	56.47	47.83	94.74	75.26
Portugal	17.35	4.44	16.33	4.26	14.29	10.42	29.59	16.33
Spain	38.14	23.53	49.02	19.75	34.44	39.39	64.36	54.37

Sweden	14.58	29.33	8.05	36.63	18.63	80.00	62.38
United Kingdom	27.08	30.68	23.33	43.43	26.73	68.69	64.00
United States	30.00	24.68	15.38	52.13	41.84	69.39	54.08
South Asia							
Bangladesh	51.22	73.91	51.16	42.50	n.a.	n.a.	n.a.
India	26.18	50.27	34.95	40.64	19.58	67.86	41.15
Pakistan	62.63	68.82	46.39	50.54	42.71	79.00	73.74
MENA							
Egypt, Arab Rep. of	30.30	56.57	33.33	31.31	32.32	57.58	85.11
Tunisia	10.20	25.00	16.33	26.09	13.04	35.42	18.60
West Bank/Gaza	29.76	40.74	23.26	14.46	13.79	58.89	48.31
Total	34.94	41.83	29.53	29.89	23.73	78.93	61.85

n.a. Not asked.
Note: Percentage of firms ranking the constraint as a "moderate" or "major" obstacle.

Table A2.3 Obstacles to Firm Financing

Economy	Collateral	Bank paperwork	High interest rates	Special connections	Banks lack money to lend	Access to foreign banks	Access to non-banks	Access to export finance	Access to lease finance	Access to credit
Eastern Europe and Central Asia										
Albania	46.09	49.64	75.71	35.71	50.36	37.21	43.80	24.30	10.75	28.35
Armenia	16.67	18.49	63.11	12.73	15.04	11.54	9.43	3.81	9.17	14.95
Azerbaijan	51.35	48.36	76.67	57.98	79.65	70.33	63.22	63.86	65.05	65.96
Belarus	45.13	36.52	76.67	18.58	41.82	21.65	16.84	7.41	26.47	19.00
Bosnia and Herzegovina	41.76	44.33	89.47	37.78	67.37	73.47	63.74	65.12	74.16	65.75
Bulgaria	70.43	72.73	61.67	48.57	42.39	36.67	22.39	41.27	37.14	30.43
Croatia	56.20	65.08	94.35	56.45	64.75	45.83	50.88	69.44	66.37	55.46
Czech Rep.	46.23	62.02	66.92	29.09	40.71	26.92	23.96	11.96	18.89	55.75
Estonia	40.65	21.77	73.98	20.66	28.21	33.01	28.70	17.65	8.20	22.83
Georgia	50.00	47.93	87.40	56.91	47.27	61.74	47.41	50.00	54.31	40.71
Hungary	43.70	43.33	66.94	36.52	17.14	17.71	30.69	14.81	17.17	34.26
Kazakhstan	64.08	46.60	81.25	37.74	37.11	29.69	43.84	41.82	52.94	43.24
Kyrgyz Rep.	68.24	64.44	94.55	59.14	65.52	40.91	41.86	51.52	58.49	57.14
Lithuania	26.88	34.62	80.39	41.76	19.54	45.95	37.68	31.25	50.60	38.00
Moldova	61.95	57.39	90.08	51.85	58.77	40.26	54.05	52.86	54.67	50.00
Poland	63.51	69.77	88.48	23.38	6.25	18.86	33.52	29.22	21.98	37.50
Romania	70.18	61.79	95.04	39.32	46.73	45.65	45.98	49.25	76.83	46.39
Russia	52.78	50.52	77.62	44.42	38.52	35.96	42.42	35.40	48.96	42.37
Slovak Rep.	32.20	48.80	84.00	35.04	63.87	35.58	53.51	40.59	23.14	46.30
Slovenia	46.77	56.00	79.20	20.97	13.33	26.02	34.96	37.19	28.69	35.25
Turkey	45.89	42.18	87.07	41.38	41.96	32.59	29.08	31.54	22.38	38.73

Ukraine	62.81	56.86	86.70	48.82	57.07	58.58	62.50	56.67	67.91	56.15
Uzbekistan	46.72	46.49	62.90	35.00	44.04	29.46	29.36	37.00	44.92	26.36

Latin America and the Caribbean

Argentina	62.37	62.50	90.63	43.96	29.55	30.68	23.08	29.23	26.92	40.66
Brazil	67.35	72.45	92.42	61.31	22.63	24.86	32.61	20.51	20.42	31.12
Belize	50.00	48.98	87.76	39.58	22.92	36.59	28.21	29.73	36.59	46.81
Bolivia	84.69	77.00	92.86	59.60	35.05	59.34	60.23	57.97	56.96	69.89
Chile	46.24	46.39	73.20	28.26	19.59	25.27	20.51	22.22	9.89	29.55
Colombia	63.27	58.59	93.00	43.88	54.55	28.09	38.20	41.79	24.18	40.82
Costa Rica	71.58	70.83	84.38	39.58	43.75	35.42	32.58	26.15	29.76	50.55
Dominican Rep.	60.75	58.72	87.16	47.66	15.60	41.51	32.38	43.84	36.96	53.64
Ecuador	68.49	66.67	94.95	64.29	87.63	56.70	51.14	47.69	41.18	70.53
El Salvador	79.41	69.61	90.20	48.00	30.00	37.36	37.78	35.06	40.66	50.52
Guatemala	75.49	71.84	90.29	51.49	78.64	52.00	57.30	49.23	39.33	66.00
Haiti	59.79	37.62	85.86	43.88	42.22	47.92	53.13	34.62	62.64	65.59
Honduras	67.03	58.24	89.13	51.16	42.50	28.79	27.14	36.67	37.50	43.42
Mexico	64.21	71.00	83.00	60.20	71.43	42.22	48.91	49.35	48.91	55.32
Nicaragua	75.26	69.07	88.54	55.32	43.82	32.56	30.59	30.77	41.77	37.21
Panama	57.58	56.12	68.04	35.71	10.31	22.11	21.98	21.79	15.46	31.63
Peru	61.39	74.76	91.09	52.00	69.61	44.44	39.77	30.26	44.32	44.33
Trinidad and Tobago	58.42	43.56	87.13	19.00	8.91	21.00	22.00	26.53	23.23	30.61
Uruguay	47.83	56.25	85.26	30.85	18.09	13.19	18.99	30.43	34.52	30.11
Venezuela, R.B. de	70.83	72.45	90.82	33.33	41.94	26.14	29.21	53.33	33.33	45.98

East Asia

Cambodia	31.89	21.67	50.00	28.86	44.75	n.a.	n.a.	n.a.	n.a.	n.a.
China	20.20	29.00	35.35	25.53	37.00	17.14	12.79	21.33	22.47	44.44
Indonesia	53.61	47.42	87.76	42.86	52.17	27.91	25.00	26.39	27.78	38.20
Malaysia	41.49	32.99	52.58	34.74	20.22	14.29	15.19	14.71	7.69	21.84

(continued on next page)

119

Table A2.3, *continued*

Economy	Collateral	Bank paperwork	High interest rates	Special connections	Banks lack money to lend	Access to foreign banks	Access to non-banks	Access to export finance	Access to lease finance	Access to credit
Philippines	56.25	40.63	84.69	45.36	38.14	34.09	26.37	26.19	32.56	36.36
Singapore	29.17	21.65	32.99	18.75	3.23	5.43	11.24	10.11	8.70	13.04
Thailand	49.35	44.61	84.24	51.24	79.39	71.67	61.90	64.86	60.61	75.34
Sub-Saharan Africa										
Botswana	42.35	27.06	46.99	22.62	2.41	16.87	20.24	18.42	11.90	25.00
Cameroon	50.00	56.52	93.88	51.06	26.67	50.00	64.29	61.54	47.37	65.91
Côte d'Ivoire	65.38	56.25	89.41	59.04	57.32	50.00	54.32	62.82	28.40	75.90
Ethiopia	70.11	56.52	62.07	32.93	25.00	64.20	55.41	52.78	58.11	50.62
Ghana	44.55	51.52	74.75	34.02	30.21	45.56	40.22	30.85	36.08	50.00
Kenya	48.54	41.18	90.10	27.72	13.73	27.45	38.78	35.00	39.00	53.40
Madagascar	53.40	79.05	95.37	77.45	56.19	63.92	60.40	76.60	73.47	92.00
Malawi	66.04	28.85	98.08	29.41	21.15	42.31	37.25	49.02	32.00	55.77
Namibia	36.67	19.10	80.46	14.29	5.49	18.89	21.84	24.69	14.77	23.86
Nigeria	40.51	42.31	84.00	35.00	32.89	52.11	47.22	51.52	35.21	55.71
Senegal	71.79	60.00	84.21	44.29	36.76	69.44	65.67	77.27	55.07	69.86
South Africa	25.22	16.24	83.90	12.07	0.85	8.55	11.21	6.14	4.35	14.16
Tanzania	69.57	57.97	81.69	42.65	29.23	56.06	65.67	68.25	59.09	66.15
Uganda	67.48	68.85	87.50	51.67	39.83	50.00	55.66	55.86	58.33	68.38
Zambia	59.74	46.75	94.67	42.67	38.67	47.30	46.48	43.06	45.33	51.32
Zimbabwe	40.32	44.26	90.98	39.34	38.33	42.98	35.77	39.83	31.15	32.50
OECD										
Canada	32.26	40.63	49.48	24.72	6.45	8.89	14.61	13.58	8.33	12.24
France	30.34	63.16	59.14	42.39	17.89	14.94	11.36	11.49	9.89	20.21

Germany	60.61	54.00	53.54	32.29	27.17	18.29	36.36	24.68	35.79	22.83
Italy	52.22	45.05	52.27	33.33	20.24	11.11	17.19	19.61	26.39	31.17
Portugal	12.63	18.75	43.75	9.38	6.19	5.26	9.38	8.89	39.58	27.08
Spain	30.00	36.27	35.64	23.76	18.09	8.33	19.48	22.58	24.71	42.71
Sweden	34.34	17.17	23.00	15.15	5.10	7.95	17.98	20.25	6.59	10.53
United Kingdom	38.14	32.65	62.24	32.63	17.53	13.75	18.07	17.57	8.25	24.74
United States	30.30	42.86	52.53	26.80	11.22	12.50	19.10	14.47	15.38	21.05
South Asia										
Bangladesh	50.00	54.55	89.36	41.03	54.05	32.26	44.83	34.62	42.42	70.97
India	50.53	50.53	81.18	34.97	18.48	22.03	23.98	25.61	20.59	32.12
Pakistan	77.78	69.00	86.73	63.92	60.00	56.84	52.17	56.67	52.17	64.52
MENA										
Egypt, Arab Rep. of	46.32	71.13	73.96	48.45	41.24	39.18	38.95	52.13	45.74	46.81
Tunisia	22.50	27.50	53.85	22.50	5.13	18.92	27.03	10.53	7.69	51.28
West Bank/Gaza	54.65	40.91	66.28	21.59	36.71	22.22	37.04	39.13	20.00	43.21
Total	51.62	49.99	77.10	39.09	35.98	34.16	35.88	35.17	34.67	42.22

n.a. Not asked.

Note: Percentage of firms ranking each constraint as "moderate" or "major" obstacle.

Table A2.4a Sources of Fixed Investment

Economy	Retained earnings	Equity	Local commercial banks	Investment funds	Foreign banks	Family/ friends	Money lenders	Supplier credit	Leasing	State
Eastern Europe and Central Asia										
Albania	77.1	0.5	1.7	1.8	1.4	6.2	3.5	2.5	1.9	7.8
Armenia	67.3	1.0	1.8	0.4	1.4	23.2	0.5	1.0	0.9	4.9
Azerbaijan	63.4	0.2	1.3	0.4	0.6	23.8	1.5	3.4	0.8	14.4
Belarus	76.6	1.4	4.6	0.2	0.3	1.0	0.1	4.3	1.1	17.9
Bosnia and Herzegovina	63.9	5.4	12.6	1.0	5.4	4.1	1.7	4.1	0.6	n.a.
Bulgaria	58.2	1.4	6.1	1.6	0.3	16.5	2.7	5.5	3.6	4.4
Croatia	54.1	4.7	16.2	0.7	4.1	4.1	2.0	8.6	0.8	4.5
Czech Rep.	62.6	0.8	7.0	0.9	3.2	10.5	4.2	3.5	3.4	7.0
Estonia	35.5	15.9	17.7	2.0	2.3	3.9	4.2	6.8	8.5	2.3
Georgia	69.6	0.7	5.9	1.3	1.3	4.5	3.8	5.2	3.4	6.8
Hungary	52.1	6.0	14.8	2.0	0.3	13.1	1.7	4.1	2.4	4.2
Kazakhstan	63.6	3.5	6.8	3.7	0.9	9.2	0.9	5.3	4.0	10.8
Kyrgyz Rep.	80.1	1.3	1.5	2.0	0.0	4.4	1.4	2.5	3.3	7.5
Lithuania	37.8	12.3	7.2	0.7	1.4	28.2	3.6	5.2	2.7	0.8
Moldova	78.9	0.3	6.8	0.6	0.5	3.2	0.5	4.9	1.7	5.9
Poland	39.6	30.5	12.7	2.9	0.4	2.1	1.9	4.3	3.8	1.4
Romania	63.2	2.4	9.7	1.7	0.7	12.8	2.2	3.3	2.0	2.1
Russia	69.6	0.9	5.4	1.3	0.2	4.7	1.7	8.7	3.5	4.0
Slovak Rep.	65.7	1.2	9.1	0.5	2.3	3.4	2.6	4.0	7.8	6.0
Slovenia	58.1	3.4	14.0	1.6	3.0	3.4	1.2	7.7	2.7	4.8
Turkey	47.1	8.3	17.6	2.5	3.3	10.7	0.9	1.2	5.0	9.8
Ukraine	69.1	2.2	6.0	1.7	0.4	6.9	2.9	7.0	1.1	4.9
Uzbekistan	71.4	3.5	4.3	1.7	1.3	1.5	0.6	5.5	3.9	9.4

Latin America and the Caribbean

Argentina	52.4	2.5	22.0	1.2	7.4	3.5	0.8	7.4	0.6	0.1
Belize	36.4	10.9	25.6	2.2	3.1	5.9	0.3	4.0	2.1	0.5
Bolivia	56.3	0.9	21.9	0.1	2.5	4.2	0.9	8.7	0.7	0.1
Brazil	35.3	4.8	18.2	1.4	3.9	4.3	0.7	9.3	4.9	1.6
Chile	43.1	0.3	29.6	0.6	6.8	0.8	0.7	7.3	1.7	1.1
Colombia	39.5	0.8	21.1	3.5	6.1	2.0	0.0	11.7	1.9	1.0
Costa Rica	60.9	1.4	12.3	1.1	4.9	3.1	1.1	7.8	0.5	1.0
Dominican Rep.	46.1	4.2	21.1	1.3	2.8	4.3	1.9	10.1	1.3	1.3
Ecuador	41.7	3.1	12.3	2.3	3.2	6.1	0.9	16.4	2.4	0.6
El Salvador	42.8	4.3	23.7	1.9	1.7	1.6	1.4	13.0	0.3	0.4
Guatemala	35.2	0.8	17.9	2.0	5.4	3.6	0.6	14.8	1.1	0.1
Haiti	57.3	1.7	10.8	8.2	0.0	7.3	2.3	2.3	1.0	3.7
Honduras	40.6	0.7	16.5	2.3	3.3	15.3	5.1	8.0	0.1	0.0
Mexico	46.2	3.5	7.5	2.9	1.1	2.5	1.7	12.3	0.6	1.7
Nicaragua	29.0	1.9	11.2	5.9	3.6	9.5	2.4	13.5	0.6	0.4
Panama	32.8	1.8	36.1	1.3	6.1	3.5	0.6	7.8	1.0	0.3
Peru	39.7	0.7	17.3	1.7	5.5	6.0	0.8	10.5	1.1	1.2
Trinidad and Tobago	25.6	15.8	35.9	2.0	1.1	2.7	0.0	14.6	0.5	0.1
Uruguay	43.3	2.4	27.1	1.4	5.2	1.4	0.4	14.8	0.4	0.5
Venezuela, R.B. de	57.5	2.6	9.4	0.7	5.4	1.5	0.5	6.5	0.6	0.3

East Asia

Cambodia	16.6	2.3	2.3	0.3	5.4	11.5	1.7	0.6	0.1	0.3
China	56.6	2.6	9.0	4.9	0.4	5.9	6.3	2.8	1.7	1.1
Indonesia	42.2	0.3	5.7	2.5	4.0	3.2	1.1	2.1	0.6	0.1
Malaysia	24.7	7.0	9.3	1.7	2.4	2.2	2.0	16.4	3.7	0.5
Philippines	50.8	1.6	14.6	3.0	2.8	7.7	0.4	10.3	1.4	0.8

(continued on next page)

123

Table A2.4a, *continued*

Economy	Retained earnings	Equity	Local commercial banks	Investment funds	Foreign banks	Family/ friends	Money lenders	Supplier credit	Leasing	State
Singapore	56.0	7.5	14.8	0.6	7.0	1.3	0.0	4.6	0.9	0.1
Thailand	40.1	3.8	27.9	1.0	5.0	10.6	2.2	3.8	1.0	n.a.
OECD										
Canada	39.9	11.9	15.2	4.2	1.9	2.7	3.5	2.4	2.1	1.9
France	45.5	6.5	8.0	0.6	1.5	6.1	1.4	6.5	3.5	1.3
Germany	43.7	18.6	15.0	2.7	1.4	2.7	6.1	3.0	1.9	5.2
Italy	13.3	3.5	21.9	1.0	2.3	1.3	2.2	5.8	3.0	0.9
Portugal	6.9	6.7	3.9	0.6	0.3	1.9	0.0	3.9	4.2	1.5
Spain	50.4	1.0	14.7	1.2	2.1	0.5	0.6	2.6	5.1	1.4
Sweden	52.2	10.5	17.6	0.3	0.9	0.6	0.8	5.6	1.4	3.4
United Kingdom	53.7	8.2	13.2	0.4	1.0	0.9	0.9	6.3	2.7	1.7
United States	31.3	5.5	13.4	8.0	0.9	3.3	3.8	5.0	4.5	1.3
South Asia										
Bangladesh	41.6	20.5	6.4	0.4	5.8	13.2	0.5	2.7	2.9	1.8
India	27.1	5.2	22.0	6.5	1.8	3.3	1.0	0.0	1.0	n.a.
Pakistan	18.1	2.8	14.3	0.4	2.8	10.3	1.6	2.3	1.5	0.3
MENA										
Egypt, Arab Rep. of	48.0	34.7	15.7	2.3	5.5	4.7	5.7	3.3	n.a.	n.a.
West Bank/Gaza	32.4	2.8	4.3	0.1	3.8	15.0	0.2	5.0	1.5	0.1
Total	48.8	4.7	13.1	1.9	2.6	6.4	1.7	6.1	2.2	3.4

n.a. Not asked.

Notes: Percentage of firms' fixed investment from each source over the last 12 months. For the Arab Republic of Egypt, the data represent parallel results for the WBES carried out by ECES.

Table A2.4b Most Important Source of Finance for African Firms

Economy	Retained earnings	Equity	Commercial banks	Investment funds	Foreign banks	Family/ friends	Money lenders	Supplier credit	Leasing
Botswana	44.55	14.85	16.83	5.00	3.96	1.98	0.99	4.95	4.95
Cameroon	46.43	17.86	8.77	0.00	1.75	3.51	0.00	5.26	1.75
Côte d'Ivoire	40.63	9.28	13.40	4.12	5.15	3.09	1.03	8.25	4.12
Ethiopia	38.10	8.65	28.85	4.76	2.86	3.81	0.00	0.00	0.00
Ghana	38.66	7.56	2.52	5.88	1.68	2.52	0.00	3.36	0.84
Kenya	45.54	8.93	18.02	5.36	4.46	0.88	0.88	4.42	0.88
Madagascar	42.48	21.24	9.65	5.31	1.77	19.64	3.54	4.39	0.88
Malawi	38.18	3.64	10.91	14.55	7.27	1.82	1.82	3.64	0.00
Namibia	33.70	8.60	19.78	7.53	4.26	2.11	0.00	2.11	3.16
Nigeria	38.71	16.13	9.68	6.45	2.15	1.08	0.00	4.30	3.23
Senegal	27.87	12.40	6.45	0.81	2.42	12.10	3.23	4.84	1.61
South Africa	58.33	9.09	15.70	2.48	1.65	0.83	0.83	3.31	0.00
Tanzania	46.99	13.25	9.64	13.25	4.82	9.64	6.02	6.02	1.20
Tunisia	26.92	13.46	7.69	3.85	3.85	0.00	1.92	0.00	1.92
Uganda	35.07	9.85	10.45	10.45	6.77	11.03	2.99	7.35	0.74
Zambia	50.00	7.23	6.10	10.71	4.76	4.76	1.19	5.95	3.57
Zimbabwe	51.16	4.69	11.63	5.43	2.33	0.78	0.00	2.33	1.55
Total	41.33	11.22	13.06	6.27	3.44	5.23	1.41	4.27	1.63

Note: Percentage of firms rating the source as most important.

125

Table A2.5 Policy Predictability—Changes in Economic and Financial Policies That Materially Affect Your Business

Economy	Economic predictability	Economy	Economic predictability
Eastern Europe and Central Asia		Guatemala	53.77
Albania	51.61	Haiti	72.34
Armenia	60.83	Honduras	39.13
Azerbaijan	25.20	Mexico	62.89
Belarus	78.23	Nicaragua	50.00
Bosnia and Herzegovina	78.00	Panama	44.44
Bulgaria	41.80	Peru	34.91
Croatia	71.20	Trinidad and Tobago	45.54
Czech Rep.	73.02	Uruguay	27.00
Estonia	61.24	Venezuela, R.B. de	73.00
Georgia	68.00	*East Asia*	
Hungary	64.84	China	24.75
Kazakhstan	86.18	Indonesia	64.29
Kyrgyz Rep.	85.00	Malaysia	38.04
Lithuania	65.77	Philippines	52.00
Moldova	79.83	Singapore	9.18
Poland	64.06	Thailand	63.66
Romania	80.17		
Russia	86.84	*OECD*	
Slovak Rep.	71.43	Canada	40.82
Slovenia	59.68	France	38.54
Turkey	43.84	Germany	56.57
Ukraine	80.89	Italy	56.84
Uzbekistan	47.54	Portugal	26.14
		Spain	51.49
Latin America and the Caribbean		Sweden	64.36
Argentina	45.45	United Kingdom	47.00
Belize	34.69	United States	34.69
Bolivia	42.42		
Brazil	71.64	*South Asia*	
Chile	25.25	India	49.28
Colombia	69.00	Pakistan	33.66
Costa Rica	35.00	*MENA*	
Dominican Rep.	50.00	West Bank and Gaza	29.21
Ecuador	66.00	Total	57.65
El Salvador	45.63		

Notes: Percentage of firms responding that changes in policies are "completely," "highly," or "fairly" unpredictable. Question not asked in Africa and MENA (except West Bank and Gaza).

Table A2.6 In the Last Three Years, the Laws, Regulations, and Policies Affecting My Business Have Become . . .

Economy	Changes in policies	Economy	Changes in policies
Eastern Europe and Central Asia		Haiti	75.28
Albania	64.00	Honduras	57.14
Armenia	83.87	Mexico	62.63
Azerbaijan	51.56	Nicaragua	63.92
Belarus	50.00	Panama	52.08
Bosnia and Herzegovina	55.10	Peru	42.59
Bulgaria	76.86	Trinidad and Tobago	24.00
Croatia	61.42	Uruguay	43.43
Czech Rep.	67.42	Venezuela, R.B. de	94.00
Estonia	43.18	*East Asia*	
Georgia	58.91	Cambodia	43.00
Hungary	61.90	China	20.62
Kazakhstan	77.17	Indonesia	64.00
Kyrgyz Rep.	76.00	Malaysia	26.32
Lithuania	85.45	Philippines	46.46
Moldova	84.00	Singapore	2.00
Poland	48.21	Thailand	32.94
Romania	72.00	*OECD*	
Russia	76.58	Canada	35.42
Slovak Rep.	70.54	France	52.58
Slovenia	44.00	Germany	73.00
Turkey	75.68	Italy	71.13
Ukraine	76.89	Portugal	45.83
Uzbekistan	43.20	Spain	29.00
Latin America and the Caribbean		Sweden	51.52
Argentina	80.41	United Kingdom	45.54
Belize	36.00	United States	48.48
Bolivia	88.00	*South Asia*	
Brazil	94.03	Bangladesh	80.00
Chile	48.45	India	54.90
Colombia	64.36	Pakistan	53.54
Costa Rica	68.00	*MENA*	
Dominican Rep.	50.45	West Bank and Gaza	35.48
Ecuador	77.66	Total	58.95
El Salvador	53.40		
Guatemala	41.90		

Notes: Percentage of firms responding "much less" or "somewhat less" predictable. Question not asked in Africa.

Table A2.7 "The Process of Developing New Rules, Regulations, or Policies Is Usually Such That Businesses Are Informed in Advance of Changes Affecting Them." Would You Say This Is True...?

Economy	Informed of changes in laws	Economy	Informed of changes in laws
Eastern Europe and Central Asia		Honduras	45.65
Albania	71.43	Mexico	58.33
Armenia	74.38	Nicaragua	78.13
Azerbaijan	26.77	Panama	44.44
Belarus	63.20	Peru	67.92
Bosnia and Herzegovina	72.45	Trinidad and Tobago	44.55
Bulgaria	58.33	Uruguay	45.45
Croatia	42.86	Venezuela, R.B. de	65.66
Czech Rep.	32.81	*Africa*	
Estonia	51.18	Botswana	10.53
Georgia	56.25	Cameroon	32.14
Hungary	73.17	Côte d'Ivoire	30.93
Kazakhstan	76.80	Ethiopia	58.42
Kyrgyz Rep.	75.68	Ghana	27.93
Lithuania	78.90	Kenya	57.80
Moldova	69.17	Madagascar	60.00
Poland	62.09	Malawi	26.42
Romania	88.52	Namibia	8.70
Russia	75.93	Nigeria	49.43
Slovak Rep.	62.02	Senegal	40.00
Slovenia	39.20	South Africa	6.78
Turkey	51.35	Tanzania	32.50
Ukraine	80.91	Uganda	38.52
Uzbekistan	50.00	Zambia	38.10
Latin America and the Caribbean		Zimbabwe	63.49
Argentina	67.00	*MENA*	
Belize	24.49	Egypt, Arab Rep. of	14.00
Bolivia	61.00	Tunisia	8.33
Brazil	60.70	West Bank and Gaza	47.83
Chile	32.00	*East Asia*	
Colombia	67.33	China	28.57
Costa Rica	40.00	Indonesia	40.40
Dominican Rep.	63.06	Malaysia	40.43
Ecuador	67.68	Philippines	22.00
El Salvador	56.31	Singapore	5.00
Guatemala	56.60	Thailand	26.60
Haiti	76.70		

(continued on next page)

Table A2.7, *continued*

Economy	Informed of changes in laws	Economy	Informed of changes in laws
OECD		United Kingdom	24.51
Canada	11.34	United States	18.18
France	28.57	*South Asia*	
Germany	49.49	Bangladesh	42.86
Italy	43.75	India	35.47
Portugal	13.64	Pakistan	45.00
Spain	49.02	Total (all responses)	49.60
Sweden	41.18		

Notes: Percentage of firms responding "never" or "seldom." Question not asked in all countries surveyed.

Table A2.8 "In Case of Important Changes in Laws or Policies Affecting My Business Operation, the Government Takes into Account Concerns Voiced Either by Me or by My Business Association." Would You Say This Is True . . . ?

Economy	Government takes into account voices of firms	Economy	Government takes into account voices of firms
Eastern Europe/Central Asia		Haiti	77.67
Albania	75.35	Honduras	61.96
Armenia	80.83	Mexico	54.74
Azerbaijan	48.74	Nicaragua	80.21
Belarus	78.86	Panama	44.90
Bosnia and Herzegovina	65.91	Peru	75.24
Bulgaria	81.36	Trinidad and Tobago	26.73
Croatia	75.00	Uruguay	60.82
Czech Rep.	56.88	Venezuela, R.B. de	53.06
Estonia	71.07	*East Asia*	
Georgia	66.67	Cambodia	49.52
Hungary	81.67	China	41.94
Kazakhstan	83.47	Indonesia	50.00
Kyrgyz Rep.	77.27	Malaysia	41.94
Lithuania	80.19	Philippines	25.25
Moldova	78.15	Singapore	13.27
Poland	73.74	Thailand	22.33
Romania	92.98	*OECD*	
Russia	87.40	Canada	43.30
Slovak Rep.	77.52	France	52.13
Slovenia	50.40	Germany	76.04
Turkey	40.54	Italy	39.36
Ukraine	88.07	Portugal	44.44
Uzbekistan	46.43	Spain	46.00
Latin America and the Caribbean		Sweden	44.44
Argentina	64.65	United Kingdom	42.00
Belize	25.53	United States	38.54
Bolivia	65.00	*South Asia*	
Brazil	50.50	Bangladesh	32.00
Chile	38.95	India	19.80
Colombia	60.40	Pakistan	34.00
Costa Rica	43.43	*MENA*	
Dominican Rep.	40.91	West Bank and Gaza	63.04
Ecuador	71.72	Total (all responses)	58.20
El Salvador	59.80		
Guatemala	62.86		

Note: Percentage of firms responding "never" or "seldom."

Table A2.9 "It Is Common for Firms in My Line of Business to Have to Pay Some Irregular 'Additional Payments' to Get Things Done."

Economy	Advance payments	Economy	Advance payments
Eastern Europe and Central Asia		Dominican Rep.	22.73
Albania	46.71	Ecuador	40.63
Armenia	40.34	El Salvador	20.59
Azerbaijan	59.32	Guatemala	27.45
Belarus	14.17	Haiti	68.69
Bosnia and Herzegovina	29.21	Honduras	32.91
Bulgaria	23.93	Mexico	30.61
Croatia	17.74	Nicaragua	33.70
Czech Rep.	26.27	Panama	21.65
Estonia	12.90	Peru	29.13
Georgia	36.84	Trinidad and Tobago	10.64
Hungary	31.25	Uruguay	15.85
Kazakhstan	23.68	Venezuela, R.B. de	36.46
Kyrgyz Rep.	26.92	*South Asia*	
Lithuania	23.16	Bangladesh	93.88
Moldova	33.33	India	54.90
Poland	32.67	Pakistan	70.30
Romania	50.86	*MENA*	
Russia	29.15	Egypt, Arab Rep. of	74.23
Slovak Rep.	34.62	Tunisia	5.260
Slovenia	7.69	West Bank and Gaza	7.780
Turkey	36.72	*Sub-Saharan Africa*	
Ukraine	35.32	Botswana	17.20
Uzbekistan	46.55	Cameroon	62.50
East Asia		Côte d'Ivoire	62.03
Cambodia	43.83	Ethiopia	48.28
Indonesia	67.68	Ghana	52.48
Malaysia	20.45	Kenya	65.09
Philippines	43.00	Madagascar	84.76
Singapore	2.02	Malawi	37.74
Thailand	78.67	Namibia	17.98
Latin America and the Caribbean		Nigeria	75.61
Argentina	31.82	Senegal	58.23
Belize	21.74	South Africa	23.28
Bolivia	46.39	Tanzania	69.33
Brazil	26.98	Uganda	69.67
Chile	4.08	Zambia	44.59
Colombia	19.39	Zimbabwe	50.43
Costa Rica	19.39		

(continued on next page)

Table A2.9, *continued*

Economy	Advance payments	Economy	Advance payments
OECD		Spain	11.58
Canada	4.21	Sweden	0.99
France	27.85	United Kingdom	5.15
Germany	19.77	United States	20.43
Italy	7.69	Total	36.34
Portugal	13.48		

Notes: Percent of firms responding "always," "mostly," or "frequently." Question not asked in China due to government censorship policies.

Table A2.10 On Average, What Percentage of Revenues Do Firms Like Yours Typically Pay Per Annum in Unofficial Payments to Public Officials?

Economy	0% (%)	<1% (%)	1–1.99% (%)	2–9.99% (%)	10–12% (%)	13–25% (%)	>25% (%)
Eastern Europe and Central Asia							
Albania	13.82	30.89	16.26	17.89	15.45	5.69	0
Armenia	0	43.75	12.50	15.63	6.25	15.63	6.25
Azerbaijan	0	19.54	36.78	10.34	20.69	5.75	6.90
Belarus	6.82	59.09	11.36	18.18	0	0	4.55
Bosnia and Herzegovina	25.00	18.75	9.38	18.75	15.63	6.25	6.25
Bulgaria	0	42.37	32.20	11.86	10.17	3.39	0
Croatia	0	55.32	27.66	17.02	0	0	0
Czech Rep.	0	43.40	16.98	20.75	15.09	1.89	1.89
Estonia	0	35.19	37.04	27.78	0	0	0
Georgia	0	9.43	18.87	30.19	26.42	15.09	0
Hungary	0	54.76	14.29	19.05	9.52	2.38	0
Kazakhstan	0	45.07	16.90	18.31	14.08	2.82	2.82
Kyrgyz Rep.	0	28.17	22.54	28.17	14.08	4.23	2.82
Lithuania	0	49.02	13.73	23.53	7.84	5.88	0
Moldova	7.58	19.70	24.24	24.24	12.12	7.58	4.55
Poland	0	59.38	20.83	13.54	6.25	0	0
Romania	2.53	27.85	35.44	22.78	7.59	2.53	1.27
Russia	0	39.53	25.30	22.13	9.09	2.37	1.58
Slovak Rep.	0	39.58	22.92	29.17	6.25	2.08	0
Slovenia	0	53.66	14.63	24.39	4.88	0	2.44
Turkey	0	55.84	16.88	18.18	3.90	3.90	1.30
Ukraine	0	26.77	16.54	29.13	16.54	6.30	4.72
Uzbekistan	0	24.32	21.62	32.43	14.86	4.05	2.70
Latin America and the Caribbean							
Argentina	52.94	8.82	10.29	17.65	8.82	1.47	0
Belize	63.41	17.07	2.44	14.63	2.44	0	0
Bolivia	28.77	15.07	10.96	30.14	8.22	6.85	0
Brazil	55.00	25.00	8.57	8.57	2.86	0	0
Chile	84.54	8.25	2.06	2.06	2.06	1.03	0
Colombia	67.03	24.18	5.49	3.30	0	0	0
Costa Rica	56.18	28.09	2.25	11.24	1.12	0	1.12
Dominican Rep.	37.37	36.36	10.10	11.11	3.03	1.01	1.01
Ecuador	42.31	14.10	7.69	16.67	12.82	2.56	3.85
El Salvador	81.52	10.87	2.17	3.26	1.09	1.09	0
Guatemala	60.00	17.65	4.71	11.76	3.53	2.35	0
Haiti	21.00	32.00	4.00	11.00	18.00	12.00	2.00
Honduras	73.86	10.23	2.27	9.09	3.41	0	1.14

(continued on next page)

Table A2.10, *continued*

Economy	0% (%)	<1% (%)	1–1.99% (%)	2–9.99% (%)	10–12% (%)	13–25% (%)	>25% (%)
Mexico	48.24	16.47	8.24	12.94	12.94	1.18	0
Nicaragua	58.89	13.33	7.78	7.78	7.78	0	4.44
Panama	62.92	24.72	2.25	6.74	0	3.37	0
Peru	45.35	19.77	6.98	16.28	8.14	3.49	0
Trinidad and Tobago	78.72	9.57	5.32	6.38	0	0	0
Uruguay	86.67	9.33	1.33	2.67	0	0	0
Venezuela, R.B. de	57.33	14.67	6.67	10.67	2.67	5.33	2.67
East Asia							
Cambodia	35.21	17.60	7.49	25.09	4.87	6.74	3.00
Indonesia	7.50	26.25	18.75	22.50	8.75	12.50	3.75
Malaysia	68.85	9.84	3.28	9.84	8.20	0	0
Philippines	39.56	26.37	17.58	8.79	6.59	1.10	0
Singapore	97.00	2.00	1.00	0	0	0	0
Thailand	9.42	26.09	18.12	25.36	13.41	5.43	2.17
OECD							
Canada	92.93	5.05	0	1.01	1.01	0	0
France	83.12	10.39	3.90	1.30	1.30	0	0
Germany	52.17	20.29	7.25	17.39	2.90	0	0
Italy	84.42	7.79	2.60	3.90	0	1.30	0
Portugal	91.67	6.25	1.04	1.04	0	0	0
Spain	91.75	7.22	1.03	0	0	0	0
Sweden	96.91	3.09	0	0	0	0	0
United Kingdom	89.16	8.43	1.20	1.20	0	0	0
United States	52.44	18.29	8.54	8.54	8.54	1.22	2.44
South Asia							
Bangladesh	20.51	25.64	25.64	12.82	5.13	10.26	0
Pakistan	17.98	16.85	16.85	22.47	17.98	5.62	2.25
MENA							
West Bank/ Gaza	78.95	10.53	0	5.26	5.26	0	0
Total	38.62	23.45	11.86	14.58	7.01	3.11	1.37

Note: Question not asked in all countries surveyed.

Table A2.11 When Firms in Your Industry Do Business with the Government, How Much of the Contract Value Would They Typically Offer in Additional or Unofficial Payments to Secure the Contract?

Region/country	0% (%)	Up to 5% (%)	6–10% (%)	11–15% (%)	16–20% (%)	>20% (%)
Africa	23.02	1.90	6.08	8.04	1.90	1.90
MENA	16.93	5.91	17.32	7.48	0.79	0
East Asia NIC/China	50.83	1.00	0.33	0	0	14.29
East Asia Dev.	10.97	10.65	7.28	2.53	2.64	6.33
South Asia	15.98	12.40	21.21	3.03	3.03	11.29
Latin America and the Caribbean	62.11	4.03	6.14	1.68	1.25	24.36
OECD	66.89	4.40	1.76	0.11	0.22	26.29
CIS	5.04	13.06	7.34	2.19	1.46	1.12
CEE	9.55	10.23	7.73	2.96	1.02	0.85
Total	28.68	7.25	6.95	3.09	1.40	9.48
Sub-Saharan Africa						
Botswana	76.24	1.98	0.99	0	0.99	1.98
Cameroon	12.28	1.75	7.02	10.53	5.26	1.75
Côte d'Ivoire	11.34	1.03	6.19	11.34	0	0
Ethiopia	28.57	3.81	8.57	2.86	0	1.90
Ghana	22.69	0.84	8.40	6.72	0	0
Kenya	16.81	1.77	3.54	14.16	3.54	2.65
Madagascar	3.45	2.59	7.76	12.93	9.48	8.62
Malawi	20.00	0	10.91	1.82	0	0
Namibia	50.53	2.11	0	0	0	0
Nigeria	3.23	1.08	8.60	20.43	4.30	2.15
Senegal	4.84	1.61	5.65	4.84	1.61	0
South Africa	54.55	0.83	3.31	2.48	0	0.83
Tanzania	22.89	2.41	9.64	8.43	0	1.20
Uganda	10.95	3.65	10.95	10.95	2.92	1.46
Zambia	10.71	1.19	4.76	13.10	1.19	4.76
Zimbabwe	17.83	2.33	3.10	7.75	0.78	2.33
MENA						
Egypt, Arab Rep. of	5.88	11.76	37.25	18.63	1.96	—
Tunisia	61.54	3.85	3.85	0	0	—
West Bank and Gaza	5.00	1.00	4.00	0	0	—
East Asia NIC						
China	n.a.	n.a.	n.a.	n.a.	n.a.	n.a.
Malaysia	57.00	3.00	1.00	—	—	39.00
Singapore	96.00	0	0	—	—	4.00

(continued on next page)

Table A2.11, *continued*

Region/country	0% (%)	Up to 5% (%)	6–10% (%)	11–15% (%)	16–20% (%)	>20% (%)
East Asia Developing						
Cambodia	0.92	0.92	1.23	0	0.92	0
Indonesia	32.00	14.00	10.00	3.00	7.00	34.00
Philippines	54.00	12.00	11.00	2.00	4.00	17.00
Thailand	3.55	17.06	10.43	4.50	2.61	2.13
South Asia						
Bangladesh	8.00	28.00	8.00	6.00	6.00	0
India	11.90	8.10	28.57	2.38	1.43	0.95
Pakistan	28.16	13.59	12.62	2.91	4.85	37.86
Latin America and the Caribbean						
Argentina	37.00	4.00	13.00	5.00	0	41.00
Belize	58.00	8.00	6.00	2.00	0	26.00
Bolivia	35.00	4.00	22.00	3.00	2.00	25.00
Brazil	48.26	5.97	4.48	2.99	1.00	37.31
Chile	85.00	4.00	1.00	0	0	10.00
Colombia	69.31	1.98	6.93	0.99	0.99	19.80
Costa Rica	70.00	6.00	2.00	1.00	0	21.00
Dominican Rep.	76.58	3.60	6.31	2.70	2.70	8.11
Ecuador	45.00	9.00	7.00	3.00	2.00	34.00
El Salvador	75.00	1.92	2.88	1.92	0.96	17.31
Guatemala	60.38	5.66	9.43	0	0.94	23.58
Haiti	54.37	0	0.97	2.91	6.80	34.95
Honduras	75.00	3.00	2.00	0	0	20.00
Mexico	57.00	4.00	14.00	2.00	0	23.00
Nicaragua	76.00	4.00	4.00	1.00	3.00	12.00
Panama	82.00	1.00	4.00	0	1.00	12.00
Peru	53.70	6.48	7.41	1.85	0	30.56
Trinidad and Tobago	81.19	1.98	0	0	0	16.83
Uruguay	70.00	3.00	0	0	1.00	26.00
Venezuela, R.B. de	44.00	3.00	11.00	2.00	2.00	38.00
OECD						
Canada	89.11	0.99	0.99	0	0	8.91
France	26.00	9.00	7.00	0	0	58.00
Germany	44.00	17.00	2.00	1.00	0	36.00
Italy	63.00	4.00	2.00	0	0	31.00
Portugal	86.00	1.00	0	0	0	13.00
Spain	72.12	1.92	1.92	0	0	24.04
Sweden	87.25	0	0	0	0	12.75
United Kingdom	71.57	1.96	1.96	0	0	21.57
United States	62.00	4.00	0	0	2.00	32.00

(continued on next page)

Table A2.11, *continued*

Region/country	0% (%)	Up to 5% (%)	6–10% (%)	11–15% (%)	16–20% (%)	>20% (%)
CIS						
Albania	18.40	12.88	10.43	6.75	3.07	3.68
Bosnia and Herzegovina	6.67	4.76	4.76	2.86	0.95	1.90
Bulgaria	0.80	4.80	9.60	0	2.40	0.80
Croatia	4.72	22.05	5.51	0.79	0	0.79
Czech Rep.	1.46	7.30	6.57	3.65	2.92	1.46
Estonia	0.76	21.21	6.82	3.03	1.52	0
Hungary	5.43	8.53	3.10	2.33	0	0
Lithuania	3.57	7.14	4.46	0	0.89	0
Poland	4.89	14.67	9.78	1.78	1.33	0.89
Romania	2.40	13.60	7.20	1.60	0	1.60
Slovak Rep.	3.10	17.83	9.30	0	3.10	1.55
Slovenia	5.60	16.80	3.20	0.80	2.40	0
Turkey	4.67	14.67	10.67	3.33	0	1.33
CEE						
Armenia	16.80	9.60	3.20	1.60	0	0
Azerbaijan	1.56	8.59	15.63	14.06	3.91	0
Belarus	12.80	6.40	0.80	0	0	0
Georgia	1.55	5.43	6.20	3.88	2.33	2.33
Kazakhstan	13.39	4.72	3.15	1.57	0	0.79
Kyrgyz Rep.	7.20	8.80	4.80	4.80	0.80	2.40
Moldova	8.80	14.40	7.20	1.60	2.40	0.80
Russia	7.81	12.76	7.24	1.71	0.38	0.76
Ukraine	5.78	10.67	13.33	1.33	1.78	0.89
Uzbekistan	28.80	12.80	12.80	4.00	0	0.80

n.a. Not asked in China because of government censorship policies.
— Data not available.

Table A2.12 Recognizing the Difficulties Many Enterprises Face in Fully Complying with Taxes and Regulations, What Percentage of Total Sales Would You Estimate the Typical Firm in Your Area of Activity Reports for Tax Purposes?

Economy	100%	90–99%	80–89%	70–79%	60–69%	50–59%	<50%
Sub-Saharan Africa							
Botswana	35.64	13.86	7.92	9.90	7.92	5.94	4.95
Cameroon	29.82	10.53	15.79	8.77	5.26	8.77	0
Côte d'Ivoire	26.80	12.37	11.34	3.09	9.28	3.09	2.06
Ethiopia	27.62	13.33	11.43	6.67	4.76	6.67	2.86
Ghana	24.37	14.29	6.72	10.08	3.36	5.88	6.72
Kenya	30.09	19.47	9.73	7.96	4.42	3.54	3.54
Madagascar	36.21	9.48	6.90	6.90	4.31	5.17	3.45
Malawi	29.09	10.91	10.91	9.09	9.09	1.82	5.45
Namibia	24.21	12.63	5.26	9.47	5.26	6.32	6.32
Nigeria	26.88	20.43	5.38	9.68	10.75	5.38	0
Senegal	22.58	11.29	8.87	7.26	9.68	7.26	1.61
South Africa	29.75	13.22	11.57	7.44	7.44	6.61	5.79
Tanzania	34.94	9.64	6.02	7.23	3.61	9.64	8.43
Uganda	31.39	14.60	11.68	8.03	4.38	4.38	2.92
Zambia	32.14	15.48	7.14	11.90	3.57	5.95	0
Zimbabwe	28.68	19.38	4.65	10.85	7.75	6.20	1.55
MENA							
Egypt, Arab Rep. of	0	7.84	5.88	14.71	30.39	28.43	12.75
Tunisia	0	34.62	0	7.69	7.69	9.62	36.54
West Bank/Gaza	13.00	11.00	11.00	7.00	3.00	12.00	11.00
East Asia NIC							
China	11.88	9.90	5.94	2.97	0.99	8.91	43.56
Malaysia	13.00	7.00	8.00	1.00	1.00	3.00	17.00
Singapore	77.00	2.00	2.00	1.00	0	1.00	5.00
East Asia Developing							
Cambodia	17.79	4.91	5.21	4.60	3.99	6.75	30.06
Indonesia	23.00	10.00	9.00	12.00	2.00	4.00	12.00
Philippines	41.00	7.00	17.00	6.00	4.00	3.00	12.00
Thailand	18.48	8.53	8.53	13.03	7.82	15.17	15.88
South Asia							
Bangladesh	12.00	2.00	8.00	8.00	8.00	28.00	12.00
India	40.95	20.95	7.14	0.95	2.86	1.90	1.43
Pakistan	21.36	8.74	2.91	3.88	5.83	16.50	18.45
Latin America and the Caribbean							
Argentina	36.00	7.00	5.00	11.00	9.00	8.00	7.00
Belize	24.00	8.00	2.00	6.00	12.00	8.00	6.00

(continued on next page)

Table A2.12, *continued*

Economy	100%	90–99%	80–89%	70–79%	60–69%	50–59%	<50%
Bolivia	20.00	9.00	11.00	9.00	10.00	12.00	16.00
Brazil	39.30	6.97	5.97	7.96	6.47	6.97	11.94
Chile	73.00	10.00	7.00	1.00	0	0	3.00
Colombia	50.50	0.99	5.94	3.96	3.96	1.98	23.76
Costa Rica	25.00	5.00	21.00	10.00	7.00	4.00	8.00
Dominican Rep.	24.32	7.21	17.12	13.51	6.31	2.70	9.91
Ecuador	24.00	5.00	15.00	7.00	9.00	8.00	17.00
El Salvador	64.42	7.69	0.96	3.85	3.85	5.77	4.81
Guatemala	31.13	5.66	7.55	7.55	8.49	7.55	13.21
Haiti	11.65	5.83	3.88	1.94	1.94	4.85	62.14
Honduras	54.00	1.00	4.00	12.00	5.00	3.00	6.00
Mexico	40.00	7.00	7.00	6.00	6.00	6.00	8.00
Nicaragua	53.00	1.00	7.00	6.00	5.00	2.00	12.00
Panama	26.00	5.00	6.00	5.00	3.00	6.00	29.00
Peru	34.26	11.11	9.26	14.81	7.41	8.33	9.26
Trinidad and Tobago	20.79	3.96	34.65	9.90	1.98	4.95	15.84
Uruguay	63.00	3.00	4.00	0	3.00	6.00	8.00
Venezuela, R.B. de	41.00	3.00	9.00	8.00	3.00	7.00	11.00
OECD							
Canada	67.33	8.91	8.91	2.97	3.96	1.98	0
France	63.00	11.00	7.00	5.00	2.00	0	1.00
Germany	12.00	13.00	29.00	10.00	5.00	6.00	2.00
Italy	67.00	7.00	1.00	3.00	3.00	0	0
Portugal	42.00	28.00	5.00	1.00	0	4.00	4.00
Spain	49.04	16.35	8.65	4.81	2.88	1.92	1.92
Sweden	46.08	25.49	3.92	2.94	0	0	1.96
United Kingdom	50.00	10.78	1.96	5.88	2.94	0.98	4.90
United States	45.00	23.00	7.00	7.00	2.00	1.00	9.00
CIS							
Albania	0	0	0	0	0	0	0
Bosnia and Herzegovina	61.9	8.57	8.57	7.62	5.71	0.95	5.71
Bulgaria	28.80	8.00	7.20	8.00	4.80	11.20	9.60
Croatia	26.77	18.11	7.09	15.75	1.57	11.02	7.87
Czech Rep.	36.50	12.41	8.76	5.11	4.38	5.11	5.11
Estonia	35.61	18.94	13.64	12.12	5.30	9.09	0.76
Hungary	42.64	11.63	12.40	10.85	7.75	3.88	4.65
Lithuania	0	0	0	0.89	0.89	6.25	17.86
Poland	43.11	16.00	10.22	8.44	6.67	4.89	3.11
Romania	36.80	20.80	24.00	8.00	3.20	4.80	2.40
Slovak Rep.	0	0	0	0	3.10	4.65	10.85

(continued on next page)

Table A2.12, *continued*

Economy	100%	90–99%	80–89%	70–79%	60–69%	50–59%	<50%
Slovenia	74.40	14.40	4.80	2.40	0.80	0.80	0.80
Turkey	20.67	11.33	13.33	6.00	4.67	14.00	12.67
CEE							
Armenia	38.40	21.60	12.00	3.20	2.40	5.60	5.60
Azerbaijan	25.78	10.94	8.59	5.47	7.81	14.06	16.41
Belarus	60.00	21.60	3.20	3.20	2.40	1.60	0.80
Georgia	38.76	3.10	10.85	3.10	8.53	5.43	6.98
Kazakhstan	43.31	3.15	10.24	6.30	3.15	8.66	5.51
Kyrgyz Rep.	16.00	19.20	43.20	4.00	7.20	8.80	0.80
Moldova	44.80	11.20	6.40	8.00	4.80	8.80	8.80
Russia	26.67	13.14	13.14	12.38	5.14	13.52	7.62
Ukraine	36.89	12.00	8.00	6.67	4.00	8.44	7.56
Uzbekistan	37.60	14.40	14.40	2.40	2.40	13.60	9.60

Table A2.13 Could You Please Rate the Overall Quality and Efficiency of Services Delivered by the Following Public Agencies or Services?

Economy	Customs	Courts	Roads	Postal	Telephone	Power	Water	Health	Military	Government	Parliament	Central bank
Eastern Europe and Central Asia												
Albania	49.28	61.72	64.94	7.55	20.13	31.06	58.86	40.82	16.36	26.62	38.57	23.14
Armenia	60.67	55.56	72.81	41.18	42.98	29.03	46.72	57.43	19.05	58.42	64.95	52.70
Azerbaijan	37.25	42.11	58.40	52.34	45.60	46.46	50.41	76.36	55.43	15.58	34.67	35.29
Belarus	46.77	55.88	37.72	8.20	33.87	8.06	16.26	41.18	17.07	45.63	50.00	52.38
Bosnia and Herzegovina	23.08	51.16	67.42	24.18	27.96	48.89	44.44	37.08	25.40	52.44	71.95	36.99
Bulgaria	24.10	33.02	83.47	26.89	28.46	30.33	33.61	47.46	11.94	28.45	47.37	26.36
Croatia	13.16	61.98	40.34	7.26	8.00	8.80	16.80	50.40	11.61	53.78	52.94	39.67
Czech Rep.	36.49	73.53	66.39	30.30	15.44	14.29	11.72	33.87	50.53	66.13	79.84	33.94
Estonia	14.95	42.42	79.53	6.87	11.45	9.23	17.74	47.24	39.02	31.67	47.06	4.31
Georgia	55.28	49.11	54.17	29.03	18.60	40.31	29.69	62.70	65.14	32.80	57.60	32.08
Hungary	29.21	51.25	46.07	14.17	9.38	4.72	10.48	40.71	25.32	54.55	61.80	15.85
Kazakhstan	59.77	55.56	69.30	29.52	32.00	26.40	23.53	72.50	57.63	55.24	66.33	40.86
Kyrgyz Rep.	72.60	70.15	80.95	30.77	36.89	38.40	35.25	76.86	54.90	67.37	75.82	67.82
Lithuania	45.21	57.35	26.14	3.77	19.82	11.93	30.61	47.87	22.64	35.29	74.71	26.80
Moldova	50.57	62.77	83.33	18.49	33.60	73.60	57.01	86.67	57.69	89.66	91.60	60.64
Poland	25.00	55.10	65.76	9.01	14.67	13.24	10.75	60.00	25.50	37.81	49.51	10.61
Romania	32.14	47.57	60.53	12.30	25.81	16.80	29.84	49.59	16.67	72.38	71.84	33.98
Russia	37.61	64.37	61.79	22.53	33.20	24.90	36.27	72.94	63.57	89.54	87.45	69.18
Slovak Rep.	39.13	51.43	42.98	16.13	18.11	11.38	8.87	63.49	13.40	41.51	61.95	18.63
Slovenia	10.17	64.17	35.83	3.20	4.80	12.00	16.39	20.97	19.33	27.87	58.20	7.50
Turkey	49.61	57.97	43.45	12.33	7.43	17.57	35.86	75.68	5.44	52.05	61.90	12.69

(continued on next page)

Table A2.13, *continued*

Economy	Customs	Courts	Roads	Postal	Telephone	Power	Water	Health	Military	Government	Parliament	Central bank
Ukraine	54.55	60.24	62.62	15.14	26.79	34.67	39.73	65.45	46.58	67.51	73.82	34.95
Uzbekistan	36.71	32.93	45.30	34.48	43.09	16.00	33.87	69.67	20.99	8.33	18.92	19.27
Latin America and the Caribbean												
Argentina	40.85	70.33	40.58	12.50	3.03	9.09	12.63	70.59	51.79	46.91	81.40	31.71
Belize	27.66	19.51	28.26	4.00	10.00	18.00	14.58	51.06	37.50	27.66	35.90	23.26
Bolivia	70.53	82.11	92.39	26.53	17.35	9.09	18.56	77.89	64.20	58.95	73.40	12.77
Brazil	58.79	73.80	65.59	4.06	n.a.	n.a.	13.07	92.39	29.81	43.50	82.74	33.33
Chile	6.19	48.42	43.16	18.75	10.20	14.43	17.53	71.43	8.79	43.01	55.32	15.46
Colombia	46.24	70.45	65.63	29.90	30.69	16.83	27.27	74.26	40.63	45.45	82.65	31.00
Costa Rica	42.55	42.55	76.53	27.55	15.00	11.00	19.39	18.37	n.a.	20.62	66.32	10.64
Dominican Rep.	27.52	47.42	47.27	25.45	3.81	86.49	47.27	80.73	23.23	13.76	61.47	4.55
Ecuador	47.31	75.53	61.70	51.02	46.46	19.00	33.00	79.38	25.77	66.67	83.51	56.25
El Salvador	12.90	47.78	39.00	37.00	13.59	21.57	31.37	58.25	28.57	31.96	57.00	18.75
Guatemala	33.67	67.71	1.90	27.72	28.57	14.42	27.72	64.71	42.05	21.15	63.16	34.95
Haiti	61.63	69.84	86.60	50.00	80.39	89.22	58.43	58.33	57.14	53.66	87.80	27.12
Honduras	35.37	57.58	51.04	37.89	30.30	37.00	38.00	64.77	53.16	26.51	44.00	28.40
Mexico	25.00	59.77	29.79	22.00	17.17	18.00	25.25	45.83	17.24	37.11	59.18	29.59
Nicaragua	39.51	62.67	53.76	14.58	13.00	24.00	28.72	73.96	29.76	53.49	60.00	36.90
Panama	16.13	42.35	25.51	31.31	26.00	36.36	29.90	58.76	n.a.	11.11	50.54	10.87
Peru	21.74	69.70	20.00	8.57	16.04	11.21	19.63	62.86	28.43	27.62	60.78	23.23
Trinidad and Tobago	15.84	6.06	41.58	23.76	15.84	16.83	52.48	66.34	10.31	22.22	25.25	5.10
Uruguay	44.09	51.19	25.35	11.36	4.00	10.00	20.43	71.64	39.58	22.89	45.45	10.00
Venezuela, R.B. de	59.14	85.71	61.22	58.16	14.29	16.00	31.31	92.93	31.03	47.96	66.67	26.88

East Asia											
Cambodia	28.40	52.35	11.48	18.62	24.79	28.71	14.61	25.54	14.48	13.24	15.60
China	14.29	20.55	11.46	14.14	14.74	12.64	30.77	n.a.	n.a.	n.a.	15.58
Indonesia	53.66	58.02	2.06	5.05	15.15	25.56	26.80	50.00	36.08	31.52	42.71
Malaysia	11.59	29.51	8.60	7.29	7.29	14.58	14.46	15.63	17.78	25.00	10.45
Philippines	35.11	27.78	24.24	14.14	14.14	32.63	32.98	19.15	40.40	29.59	20.62
Singapore	1.09	0	0	0	2.02	0	2.06	1.10	1.16	1.16	1.11
Thailand	28.76	20.26	6.31	15.89	17.52	20.42	28.42	19.86	39.59	45.17	43.90
Sub-Saharan Africa											
Botswana	12.22	6.45	18.56	14.00	11.11	7.07	18.56	4.44	4.12	11.70	n.a.
Cameroon	54.00	72.00	63.27	70.59	72.00	87.76	74.00	36.84	37.50	38.24	n.a.
Côte d'Ivoire	59.09	57.95	26.14	25.61	8.54	18.75	63.74	44.44	33.33	44.59	n.a.
Ethiopia	35.35	52.75	8.82	22.77	31.37	35.92	61.39	2.41	21.59	31.71	n.a.
Ghana	20.37	15.89	22.02	22.86	23.36	27.78	28.30	20.00	17.31	15.53	n.a.
Kenya	54.13	73.83	69.64	80.00	54.95	87.39	90.09	31.00	75.93	66.67	n.a.
Madagascar	60.19	78.50	33.33	15.04	24.56	62.04	90.18	53.85	63.89	79.82	n.a.
Malawi	28.30	30.00	37.25	71.15	67.31	36.54	74.07	28.00	40.38	39.22	n.a.
Namibia	19.10	12.64	8.79	5.38	1.08	3.23	32.61	31.58	12.36	13.64	n.a.
Nigeria	49.44	32.95	62.64	66.30	90.22	80.00	68.13	70.00	26.74	38.67	n.a.
Senegal	24.73	27.16	4.55	4.21	69.41	63.64	43.82	4.88	37.50	58.54	n.a.
South Africa	27.35	27.50	35.54	14.88	2.48	5.79	75.00	34.48	11.76	21.67	n.a.
Tanzania	36.36	42.25	30.26	26.58	44.87	81.01	67.90	8.70	10.53	24.66	n.a.
Uganda	43.32	42.74	23.85	31.75	69.53	32.56	58.33	24.14	13.95	13.18	n.a.
Zambia	14.29	29.87	48.15	33.75	27.50	42.86	69.51	36.92	37.97	48.10	n.a.
Zimbabwe	59.48	31.09	40.00	74.80	49.61	51.20	85.71	59.46	91.06	85.37	n.a.
OECD											
Canada	7.06	13.19	10.00	7.07	3.06	5.21	27.27	8.99	17.17	16.84	8.79
France	15.87	36.11	26.04	18.37	14.77	19.48	17.57	27.66	44.07	51.02	23.44

(continued on next page)

Table A2.13, *continued*

Economy	Customs	Courts	Roads	Postal	Telephone	Power	Water	Health	Military	Government	Parliament	Central bank
Germany	46.88	46.81	47.87	34.02	22.45	20.00	15.00	23.16	49.37	70.71	57.73	40.00
Italy	39.13	79.07	72.97	57.00	27.00	7.00	25.27	71.76	34.57	42.17	62.07	14.77
Portugal	14.06	52.27	45.45	15.46	51.55	23.71	15.63	35.79	7.06	24.21	38.04	14.13
Spain	16.33	32.31	20.63	30.30	22.77	11.11	8.51	19.12	5.13	13.24	28.07	13.11
Sweden	12.50	22.50	32.22	19.61	20.59	5.94	7.22	39.13	33.33	62.82	51.22	10.13
United Kingdom	11.94	38.60	58.90	13.13	8.00	10.31	15.63	21.95	1.96	41.86	48.10	25.64
United States	32.31	50.55	45.74	19.19	19.19	13.13	14.29	36.17	22.39	62.37	62.22	32.35
South Asia												
Bangladesh	53.19	27.27	48.94	37.78	56.25	69.39	50.00	81.82	7.14	72.97	66.67	50.00
India	40.00	28.34	68.53	n.a.	26.24	40.30	29.63	48.17	8.94	40.35	60.24	n.a.
Pakistan	57.29	51.52	28.09	20.39	20.59	51.96	52.08	80.21	11.24	26.44	56.14	12.22
MENA												
Egypt, Arab Rep.	5.10	7.22	7.92	6.93	3.96	2.97	7.92	21.57	2.04	4.00	8.16	n.a.
Tunisia	10.64	6.67	2.13	2.04	0	0	10.64	8.51	0	0	4.65	n.a.
West Bank/Gaza	28.57	51.47	41.76	10.99	9.78	20.88	21.35	48.15	24.36	n.a.	26.58	n.a.
Total	35.11	47.93	50.64	21.83	23.64	25.36	29.34	54.58	29.41	41.96	53.11	29.24

n.a. Not asked.

Note: Percentage of firms rating agencies as "bad," "very bad," or "slightly bad."

Table A2.14 Court Qualities: In Resolving Business Disputes, Do You Believe Your Country's Court System to Be...?

Economy	Fair	Honest	Quick	Affordable	Consistent	Enforceable
Eastern Europe and Central Asia						
Albania	63.5	25.2	84.1	80.9	82.9	88.7
Armenia	86.3	91.3	86.1	67.6	88.0	57.4
Azerbaijan	43.0	48.0	67.3	66.7	72.6	60.8
Belarus	61.5	72.8	69.5	48.4	66.0	47.9
Bosnia and Herzegovina	54.0	59.2	86.7	66.7	65.9	74.1
Bulgaria	71.2	78.7	92.0	48.1	67.3	27.6
Croatia	72.2	72.4	95.2	73.0	74.6	70.2
Czech Rep.	70.6	79.8	99.2	61.1	73.0	67.9
Estonia	35.5	32.7	82.8	45.9	47.3	46.0
Georgia	76.7	77.9	75.9	58.4	75.2	65.2
Hungary	34.7	34.4	86.5	44.0	44.9	51.0
Kazakhstan	75.5	81.7	78.8	54.0	84.2	76.0
Kyrgyz Rep.	92.0	83.2	81.3	74.7	81.4	81.7
Lithuania	79.1	88.8	94.1	66.3	83.1	61.9
Moldova	79.8	82.7	83.5	69.6	82.4	71.3
Poland	54.5	55.7	94.0	92.0	64.5	64.5
Romania	58.1	69.6	86.2	53.3	64.9	47.0
Russia	81.1	84.2	88.5	57.1	81.8	79.5
Slovak Rep.	58.0	67.5	88.5	50.8	70.4	45.0
Slovenia	33.6	37.8	90.3	77.5	40.2	24.2
Turkey	46.2	55.2	91.0	59.0	60.7	51.4
Ukraine	76.0	83.7	81.7	53.1	77.9	71.6
Uzbekistan	46.0	68.0	54.6	34.7	54.2	33.1
Latin America and the Caribbean						
Argentina	78.4	70.2	98.0	73.2	85.3	62.1
Belize	31.3	37.5	79.2	38.3	44.7	50.0
Bolivia	91.9	93.8	100.0	82.7	93.9	84.9
Brazil	62.8	64.4	97.5	84.3	77.0	52.3
Chile	35.4	30.3	92.8	47.4	46.9	30.9
Colombia	70.4	80.4	100.0	76.1	87.6	73.2
Costa Rica	35.7	40.6	92.9	44.3	52.6	54.6
Dominican Rep.	73.2	71.3	90.0	69.7	80.6	64.5
Ecuador	85.0	77.0	94.0	73.7	90.5	81.0
El Salvador	80.2	84.5	93.1	74.0	87.8	76.0
Guatemala	84.0	79.4	90.2	65.4	83.8	83.2
Haiti	89.9	91.1	97.9	74.7	94.4	90.9
Honduras	73.3	77.5	88.0	49.4	76.5	77.0
Mexico	78.6	86.6	93.9	70.2	86.7	78.6
Nicaragua	89.1	87.5	93.5	80.0	83.3	78.9
Panama	70.1	73.2	93.9	74.7	74.5	57.7

(continued on next page)

Table A2.14, *continued*

Economy	Fair	Honest	Quick	Affordable	Consistent	Enforceable
Peru	91.5	92.6	99.1	77.4	95.3	79.4
Trinidad and Tobago	23.0	29.7	91.1	85.2	67.3	61.4
Uruguay	58.5	17.6	95.8	48.8	50.0	31.5
Venezuela, R.B. de	83.7	91.5	97.0	89.0	95.0	76.8
South Asia						
Bangladesh	45.7	52.2	89.1	56.5	58.7	61.7
India	21.4	30.3	88.1	63.5	42.9	44.8
Pakistan	43.0	43.0	62.4	56.4	52.0	44.1
East Asia						
Cambodia	76.2	79.5	77.0	80.7	n.a.	58.8
China	34.4	44.0	58.2	34.1	38.6	34.5
Indonesia	89.4	93.5	94.7	79.8	89.3	83.9
Malaysia	37.2	40.5	62.9	50.6	43.0	40.5
Philippines	55.6	64.7	86.9	80.6	70.7	65.3
Singapore	0	0	9.2	28.6	7.1	2.0
Thailand	30.8	32.8	78.8	65.7	36.4	50.7
Sub-Saharan Africa						
Botswana	6.4	6.4	54.4	33.3	12.1	12.2
Cameroon	84.6	86.3	96.1	84.0	84.3	67.3
Côte d'Ivoire	67.4	76.7	96.6	76.8	77.7	69.8
Ethiopia	58.4	64.4	89.9	40.7	69.4	48.3
Ghana	46.2	54.0	83.3	50.0	59.0	47.0
Kenya	70.6	82.8	94.9	62.0	83.0	70.0
Madagascar	84.3	84.0	98.8	83.1	91.4	77.8
Malawi	47.6	52.5	90.0	45.0	52.5	57.5
Namibia	4.4	5.9	63.2	40.3	17.9	19.4
Nigeria	61.4	69.8	90.6	57.1	68.6	52.3
Senegal	51.8	54.9	84.0	70.2	65.2	48.0
South Africa	5.1	7.6	84.8	58.6	23.9	28.2
Tanzania	50.9	65.5	89.3	45.5	64.3	50.0
Uganda	67.3	75.3	89.3	64.7	76.5	69.9
Zambia	50.0	45.5	89.4	59.4	67.2	54.7
Zimbabwe	22.6	28.5	83.7	54.8	46.3	43.6
OECD						
Canada	28.6	20.4	62.9	74.7	37.5	24.5
France	52.0	39.2	91.0	64.3	48.5	24.7
Germany	53.1	47.4	90.7	90.7	74.0	72.6
Italy	60.7	59.0	97.7	85.0	77.7	68.4
Portugal	50.0	33.7	89.8	79.6	54.0	57.0

(continued on next page)

Table A2.14, *continued*

Economy	Fair	Honest	Quick	Affordable	Consistent	Enforceable
Spain	69.2	55.9	92.8	76.0	75.5	42.7
Sweden	23.2	15.2	83.0	53.1	32.0	50.5
United Kingdom	40.2	21.6	88.8	88.9	60.0	44.0
United States	59.6	55.6	83.8	85.9	71.7	57.6
MENA						
Egypt, Arab Rep. of	8.1	6.1	30.3	13.1	13.3	14.1
Tunisia	10.6	8.3	30.4	20.5	10.9	6.5
West Bank/Gaza	50.0	52.5	75.3	36.8	51.9	58.5
Total	57.1	58.5	84.6	64.0	64.9	57.2

Note: Percentage of firms choosing "seldom" or "never."

Table A2.15 How Would You Generally Rate the Efficiency of Government in Delivering Services?

Economy	Government efficiency	Economy	Government efficiency
Eastern Europe and Central Asia		Guatemala	41.90
Albania	64.00	Haiti	75.28
Armenia	83.87	Honduras	57.14
Azerbaijan	51.56	Mexico	62.63
Belarus	50.00	Nicaragua	63.92
Bosnia and Herzegovina	55.10	Panama	52.08
Bulgaria	76.86	Peru	42.59
Croatia	61.42	Trinidad and Tobago	24.00
Czech Rep.	67.42	Uruguay	43.43
Estonia	43.18	Venezuela, R.B. de	94.00
Georgia	58.91	*East Asia*	
Hungary	61.90	China	20.62
Kazakhstan	77.17	Indonesia	64.00
Kyrgyz Rep.	76.00	Malaysia	26.32
Lithuania	85.45	Philippines	46.46
Moldova	84.00	Singapore	2.00
Poland	48.21	Thailand	32.94
Romania	72.00	*OECD*	
Russia	76.58	Canada	35.42
Slovak Rep.	70.54	France	52.58
Slovenia	44.00	Germany	73.00
Turkey	75.68	Italy	71.13
Ukraine	76.89	Portugal	45.83
Uzbekistan	43.20	Spain	29.00
Latin America and the Caribbean		Sweden	51.52
Argentina	80.41	United Kingdom	45.54
Belize	36.00	United States	48.48
Bolivia	88.00	*South Asia*	
Brazil	94.03	Bangladesh	80.00
Chile	48.45	India	54.90
Colombia	64.36	Pakistan	53.54
Costa Rica	68.00	*MENA*	
Dominican Rep.	50.45	West Bank and Gaza	35.48
Ecuador	77.66	Total	58.95
El Salvador	53.40		

Notes: Percentage of firms rating government service delivery as "mostly inefficient," "inefficient," or "very inefficient." Question not asked in all countries surveyed.

Notes

1. For in-depth discussion of the path out of poverty, see Pfeffermann 2000.
2. Although indicators are useful for composing an overall snapshot of country conditions, the reader is reminded of the general disclaimer: Given inherent error margins associated with any single survey results, it is inappropriate to use the results from this survey for precise country rankings in any particular dimension of the investment climate or governance.
3. Several works known to be based on the WBES are included in the bibliography that appears at the back of this book.
4. To complement this book, we also have developed an interactive Web tool by which to access the data in a manner tailored to each user's needs. The dataset and one version of this interactive tool are on the CD-ROM enclosed with this volume. The dataset at the site http://www.worldbank.org/private sector/ic/resources/index.htm can also be downloaded and used in analyses that go far beyond what is presented here. An interactive Web tool supporting country-specific comparisons of responses to individual questions can be found at http://info.worldbank.org/governance/wbes/.
5. For a more in-depth analysis of size effects, see Schiffer and Weder 2001 (http://www.ifc.org/economics/pubs/dp43/dp43.pdf).
6. This identification may be related to a "threshold effect," in which obstacles may not constrain entry so much as they deter growth from small to medium size. As Brian Levy (1993, pp. 74–75) explains, "The *threshold burden* comprises a discontinuity in the structure of costs that results where some fiscal or bureaucratic burden is imposed only on firms above a minimum size. This discontinuity can lead some firms to rein in expansion—or to expand inefficiently by creating quasi-independent enterprises, each smaller than the threshold at which the tax and regulatory requirements are imposed."
7. Even the qualified generalizations provided above require caution when we study a particular country or region.
8. The subcontractor carrying out the survey in China could ask only this general constraint question about corruption; therefore, no further data were obtained from detailed questions on this topic.
9. See Kaufmann, Kraay, and Zoido-Lobatón 2002.

10. Governance here refers primarily to the degree of corruption, as well as qualities of the state in underpinning markets, such as transparency, fairness, accountability, efficiency, and effectiveness.

11. Readers may access the core dataset of WBES on the CD-ROM included with this book.

12. For more information on the WDR 1997 survey, see Brunetti, Kisunko, and Weder 1997a.

13. The WBES Steering Committee consisted of the authors and Luke Haggarty, Homi Kharas, Shyam Khemani, and Guy Pfeffermann.

14. For example, Dun and Bradstreet and Kompass, databases widely used for business survey sampling in Western Europe and North America, have much poorer coverage in terms of the proportion of businesses they include and the level of information offered on each company.

15. Because, by design, farmers were not included in the sample, agriculture includes either agro-industry or commercial aspects of the industry. Many more agriculture firms appear in the Africa sample, in which firms normally self-identified the sector rather than being guided by a trained surveyor.

16. Cooperatives were most common in Belarus (40 percent of firms interviewed), the Kyrgyz Republic (24 percent), and Moldova (22 percent).

17. Because much of the Africa sample was based on a mail response, this result may reflect in part a self-selection bias in responses.

18. For related econometric treatment of this potential kvetch perception bias in analyzing survey data based on subjective assessment, see also Kaufmann and Wei (1999) and Hellman and others (2000). Econometric details appear in Kaufmann, Mastruzzi, and Zavaleta (forthcoming) and Hellman and others (2000).

19. For more information, see the Investment Climate Website at http://www.worldbank.org/privatesector/ic/index.htm.

Bibliography and References

The word "processed" describes informally produced works that may not be available commonly through libraries.

Batra, Geeta, and Hong Tan. Forthcoming. "Interfirm Linkages and Total Factor Productivity Growth in Malaysian Manufacturing." Washington D.C.: World Bank.

Brunetti, Aymo, Gregory Kisunko, and Beatrice Weder. 1997a. "Institutional Obstacles to Doing Business: Region-by-Region Results from a Worldwide Survey of the Private Sector." World Bank Policy Research Working Paper 1759. Washington, D.C.

———. 1997b. "Credibility of Rules and Economic Growth: Evidence from a Worldwide Survey of the Private Sector." World Bank Policy Research Working Paper 1760. Washington, D.C.

——— 1997c. "Institutions in Transition: Reliability of Rules and Economic Performance in Former Socialist Countries." World Bank Policy Research Working Paper 1809. Washington, D.C.

Campos, J. E., D. Lien, and S. Pradhan. 1999. "The Impact of Corruption on Investment: Predictability Matters." *World Development* 27 (6): 1059–67.

Carlin, Wendy, Steven Fries, Mark Schaffer, and Paul Seabright. 2001. "Competition and Enterprise Performance in Transition Economies: Evidence from a Cross-Country Survey." EBRD Working Paper 63. London.

Clarke, George R. 1999. "Bridging the Digital Divide: How Enterprise Ownership and Foreign Competition Affect Internet Access in Eastern Europe and Central Asia." World Bank Policy Research Working Paper 2629. Washington, D.C.

Clarke, George R., Robert Cull, and Maria Soledad Martinez Peria. 2001. "Does Foreign Bank Penetration Reduce Access to Credit in Developing Countries?

Evidence from Asking Borrowers." World Bank Policy Research Working Paper 2716. Washington, D.C.

European Bank for Reconstruction and Development (EBRD). 1999. *Transition Report, 1999.* London.

Friedman, E., Simon Johnson, Daniel Kaufmann, and Pablo Zoido-Lobatón. 2000. "Dodging the Grabbing Hand: The Determinants of Unofficial Activity in 69 Countries." *Journal of Public Economics* (June).

Hellman, Joel S., and Daniel Kaufmann. 2001. "Confronting the Challenge of State Capture in Transition Economies." *Finance and Development* 38 (3),International Monetary Fund, Washington, D.C. http://www.imf.org/external/pubs/ft/fandd/2001/09/hellman.htm

Hellman, Joel S., Geraint Jones, and Daniel Kaufmann. 2000a. "'Seize the State, Seize the Day:' State Capture, Corruption, and Influence in Transition." World Bank Policy Research Working Paper 2444. Washington, D.C. http://www.worldbank.org/wbi/governance/pubs/seizestate.htm

————. 2003. "Far from Home: Do Foreign Investors Import Higher Standards of Governance in Transition Economies?" World Bank Policy Research Working Paper 2563. Washington, D.C. http://www.worldbank.org/wbi/governance/pubs/farfromhome.htm

Hellman, Joel S., Geraint Jones, Daniel Kaufmann, and Mark Schankerman. 2000. "Measuring Governance, Corruption, and State Capture: How Firms and Bureaucrats Shape the Business Environment in Transit." World Bank Policy Research Working Paper 2312. Washington, D.C. http://www.worldbank.org/wbi/governance/pubs/aggindicators.htm

Johnson, Simon, Daniel Kaufmann, and Andrei Shleifer. 1997. "The Unofficial Economy in Transition." Brookings Papers on Economic Activity (2). Washington, D.C.

Johnson, Simon, Daniel Kaufmann, and Pablo Zoido-Lobatón. 1999. "Corruption, Public Finances and the Unofficial Economy." World Bank Policy Research Working Paper 2169. Washington, D.C.

Kaufmann, Daniel, Aart Kraay, and Pablo Zoido-Lobatón. 2000. "Governance Matters: From Measurement to Action." *Finance and Development,* International Monetary Fund, Washington, D.C. http://www.imf.org/external/pubs/ft/fandd/2000/06/kauf.htm

————. 2002. "Governance Matters II: Updated Indicators for 2000/01." World Bank Policy Research Working Paper 2172. Washington, D.C. http://www.worldbank.org/wbi/governance/pubs/govmatters2001.htm

Kaufmann, Daniel, Massimo Mastruzzi, and Diego Zavaleta. Forthcoming. "Sustained Macroeconomic Reforms with Meager Growth: A Governance Puzzle in Bolivia?" In D. Rodrik, ed., *In Search of Prosperity: Analytic Narratives on Economic Growth*. Princeton, N.J.: Princeton University Press.

Kaufmann, Daniel, and S. J. Wei. 1999. "Does Grease Money Speed Up the Wheels of Commerce?" National Bureau of Economic Research Working Paper 7093 (April). Washington, D. C.

Klitgaard, Robert. 1988. *Controlling Corruption*. Berkeley: University of California Press.

Levy, Brian. 1993. "Obstacles to the Development of Indigenous Small and Medium Enterprises in Sri Lanka and Tanzania: An Empirical Assessment." *World Bank Economic Review* 7 (1): 65–83.

Levy, Brian, and Andrew Stone. 1993. "What's Holding Firms Back? Ask Them." World Bank Outreach #7, Policy Views from the Country Economics Department (January). Washington, D.C.

Lora, Eduardo, Patricia Corés, and Ana Maria Herrera. 2001. "Los Obstaculos al desarollo empresarial y el tamaño de las firmas en América Latina." Inter-American Development Bank Working Paper 447 (March). Washington, D.C.

Mauro, Paulo. 1997. "Why Worry about Corruption." *Economic Issues* number 6, International Monetary Fund, Washington, D.C. http://www.imf.org/external/pubs/ft/issues6/issue6.pdf

Nagarajan, Nithya, and others. 2001. "Perceptions of the Investment Climate: Foreign vs. Domestic Investors." Foreign Investment Advisory Service. Washington, D.C. Processed.

Pfeffermann, Guy, Gregory Kisunko, and Mariusz Sumlinski. 1999. "Trends in Private Investments in Developing Countries and Perceived Obstacles to Doing Business." IFC Economics Department Discussion Paper 37 (May). Washington, D.C.

Pfeffermann, Guy. 2000. *Paths Out of Poverty: The Role of Private Enterprise in Developing Countries*. International Finance Corporation, Washington, D.C. http://www.ifc.org/publications/paths_out_of_poverty.pdf.

Pissarides, Francesca. 2001. "Financial Structures to Promote Private Sector Development in South-Eastern Europe." EBRD Working Paper 64. London.

Roberts, Mark, and James Tybout, eds. 1996. *Industrial Evolution in Developing Countries: Micro Patterns of Turnover, Productivity and Market Structure*. New York: Oxford University Press.

Rose-Ackerman, Susan. 1978. *Corruption: A Study in Political Economy.* New York: Academic Press.

Schiffer, Mirjam, and Beatrice Weder. 2001. "Firm Size and the Business Environment: Worldwide Survey Results." IFC Discussion Paper 43. Washington, D.C. http://www.ifc.org/economics/pubs/dp43/dp43.pdf

Shleifer, Andrei, and Robert W. Vishny. 1994 "Politicians and Firms." *Quarterly Journal of Economics* 109(November): 995–1025.

Stone, Andrew H. W. 2002. "Listening to Firms: How to Use Firm-Level Surveys to Assess Constraints on Private Sector Development." World Bank Policy Research Working Paper 923. Washington, D.C.

World Bank. 1997. *World Development Report 1997: "The State in a Changing World."* Washington, D.C.: World Bank Group.

World Bank. 2000. *World Development Report 2000/2001: Attacking Poverty.* New York: Oxford University Press/World Bank.